Survey of Harm to Cooperators:
Final Report

*Prepared for the Court Administration and Case Management Committee,
the Committee on Defender Services, and the Criminal Law Committee
of the Judicial Conference of the United States*

Margaret S. Williams, Donna Stienstra, and Marvin Astrada

Federal Judicial Center

2016

This Federal Judicial Center publication was undertaken in furtherance of the Center's statutory mission to develop and conduct research and education programs for the judicial branch. While the Center regards the content as responsible and valuable, it does not reflect policy or recommendation of the Board of the Federal Judicial Center.

Contents

Acknowledgments, v

Executive Summary, 1

Introduction, 2

Survey Implementation and Administration, 3

Analysis of Results, 6

   Harm or Threat to Defendants/Offenders, 8

      Types of harm or threat to defendants/offenders, 9

      Location of the defendant/offender at the time of harm or threat, 10

      Protective custody, 12

      Sources for identifying defendants/offenders, 12

      Additional instances of harm or threat to defendants/offenders, 14

      Summary of results on harm or threat to defendants/offenders, 15

   Harm or Threat to Witnesses, 15

      Types of harm or threat to witnesses, 16

      Location of witnesses at the time of harm or threat, 17

      Sources for identifying witnesses, 18

      Additional instances of harm or threat to witnesses, 20

      Summary of results on harm or threat to witnesses, 20

   Additional Questions, 21

      Defendant/offender requests for court documents or docket sealing, 21

      Withdrawing or refusing cooperation, 22

      Comparing the frequency of harm or threat in 2014 to 2013, 25

      District steps to protect cooperating information, 25

      Open-ended comments summary, 26

Conclusion, 29

Appendix A: Survey Invitation and Questionnaires, 33

Appendix B: Other Types of Harm or Threat to Defendants, 63

Appendix C: Other Locations at the Time of Harm or Threat to Defendants, 65

Appendix D: Other Sources to Identify Defendants, 67

Appendix E: Other Types of Harm or Threat to Witnesses, 77

Appendix F: Other Locations at the Time of Harm or Threat to Witnesses, 79

Appendix G: Other Sources to Identify Witnesses, 85

Appendix H: Other Steps to Protect Cooperation Information, 91

Appendix I: Open-Ended Comments, 93

Acknowledgments

The authors thank the following individuals for their assistance with this project: Judge Julie Robinson (D. Kan.), Judge Terry Hodges (M.D. Fla.), Judge Catherine Blake (D. Md.), Judge Irene Keeley (N.D. W. Va.), and Judge Roger Titus (D. Md.); Matthew Roland, Geoff Cheshire, Cait Clarke, John Fitzgerald, Mark Miskovsky, Michelle Gardner, Jane MacCracken, and Sean Marlaire (Administrative Office of the U.S. Courts); Jim Eaglin and David Rauma (Federal Judicial Center); and David Smith (Executive Office for U.S. Attorneys).

Executive Summary

In March 2015, pursuant to an August 2014 request made to the Federal Judicial Center, we surveyed federal district judges, U.S. Attorney's Offices, federal defenders, Criminal Justice Act (CJA) district panel representative's offices, and chief probation and pretrial services offices about harm or threat of harm to government cooperators. We summarize the results of the survey below.

- Respondents were asked to report harm to defendants/offenders and witnesses in the past three years for up to five cases. We limited the number of cases to five to prevent overtaxing respondents.
- Of 1,371 recipients, 976 completed the survey—a response rate of 71%.
- Respondents reported a minimum of 571 instances of harm to defendants/offenders and witnesses. Cases often involved harm to both defendants/offenders and witnesses.
- Among all types of harm or threat, respondents most often reported threats of physical harm to defendants/offenders or witnesses and to friends or family of defendants/offenders or witnesses.
- Defendants were most likely to be harmed or threatened when in some type of custody, while witnesses were either in pretrial detention or not in custody at the time of harm or threat.
- Respondents frequently reported court documents or court proceedings as the source for identifying cooperators.
- Respondents reported that concerns of harm or threat affected the willingness of both defendants/offenders and witnesses to cooperate with the government in the past three years.
- Respondents generally agreed that harm to cooperators was a significant problem and that more needed to be done, by the judiciary and/or the Bureau of Prisons, to protect cooperators from harm.

Introduction

In August 2014, Judge Julie Robinson, then chair of the Court Administration and Case Management Committee (CACM), asked the Federal Judicial Center (FJC) to conduct a study to determine the number of offenders harmed or threatened with harm because they cooperated, or were suspected of cooperating, with the government. The population of concern included inmates who were post-conviction and in the custody of the Bureau of Prisons (BOP) and identified as cooperators through the use of court documents.[1] The request, made on behalf of CACM, the Criminal Law Committee, and the Committee on Defender Services, asked that we survey federal defenders, Criminal Justice Act (CJA) panel attorneys, federal prosecutors, and probation officers and ask them to report the number of offenders harmed or threatened with harm. We added district judges, witnesses, pretrial services offices, and pretrial detention to the study design as a result of early discussions with staff from the Administrative Office of the U.S. Courts (AO staff).

After receiving feedback from the three requesting committees, the Executive Office for U.S. Attorneys (EOUSA), and AO staff, the FJC designed a research study involving Web surveys of the groups listed above. The design of the survey instrument included asking the same basic questions of all groups, with additional questions targeted to specific populations based on which ones were most likely to have the information sought. The need to target questions to specific groups resulted in multiple versions of the survey instrument (see below). The FJC worked closely with the CACM Privacy Subcommittee (Subcommittee) to develop questionnaires that would acquire the needed information and be understood by recipients.

The Subcommittee approved the questionnaires on February 24, 2015.[2] The five groups surveyed included all chief district judges, all district judges (active and senior status), U.S. Attorney's Offices, federal public defender and CJA district panel representative's offices, and chief probation and pretrial services offices. We obtained email lists for each group from various sources, including staff of the AO and EOUSA, as well as electronically available sources. Several groups made efforts to alert respondents to the survey before the initial mailing. In September 2014, Judge Julie Robinson, Judge Catherine Blake, and Judge Irene Keeley, as chairs of their respective committees, sent an initial letter to all district judges alerting them to the problem of harm to cooperators. Several other groups made efforts to alert respondents to the study at the end of February 2015, days before the survey went into the field. The EOUSA sent an email to all U.S. attorneys alerting them to the importance of their participation in the survey. The probation and pretrial services office of the AO included notification of the survey in a weekly email to all probation and pretrial services chiefs. Judge Terry Hodges, the chair of CACM, sent a letter to all circuit chief judges asking for their help in alerting judges in their circuits to the forthcoming survey invitation. Lastly, staff from the defender services office of the AO

---

1. Letter from Judge Julie A. Robinson, chair of the Committee on Court Administration and Case Management, to Judge Jeremy D. Fogel, director of the Federal Judicial Center, August 14, 2014.

2. We asked the initial set of questions, regarding cases involving harm and the details of that harm, of all respondents, with slight variations in wording. For most respondents, we referred to "defendants and/or witnesses" while for chief probation and pretrial services offices we referred to "defendants/offenders and/or witnesses." We use these terms interchangeably in this report.

mentioned the survey to participants at their federal defender meeting prior to survey distribution.

Survey Implementation and Administration

On March 3, 2015, we distributed the surveys electronically. A cover email, signed by the chairs of the three requesting committees, explained the purpose of the survey and included the link for completing the survey.[3] Two weeks later, we sent a reminder email to everyone who had not completed the survey. We sent a final reminder email on March 31, 2015, to everyone who had not yet completed the survey. The survey closed on April 8, 2015, although anyone asking to submit a late response was permitted to do so until we began drafting the report.[4]

A few issues pertaining to survey administration merit consideration before we present our analysis of the results. First, while chief district judges and district judges responded to the surveys for themselves, the other three groups of respondents reported for their offices. The efforts to coordinate office-wide responses made completion of the survey more difficult for these groups. Moreover, the results for all judges represent the experience of individual judges over the past three years, while the results for the other groups represent the experiences of an unknown, but substantially larger, number of people for that same period. If more harm is reported by the office respondents, this should not be considered an indication of anything more than inclusion of the responses of more people. These differences in respondent groups should be kept in mind as the results are discussed below.[5]

The overall response rates, shown below in Table 1, are quite strong. Chief probation and pretrial services offices responded at the highest rate, while district judges and U.S. Attorney's Offices responded at relatively lower rates, but still at levels sufficient for analysis.

---

3. We provide a copy of this email and final versions of the survey in Appendix A. Because of an error in the survey software provided by the vendor, only half of the district judges received the email invitation on March 3. The remaining judges received the initial request for the survey on March 17, 2015. To ensure that these judges had ample time to complete the survey, we extended the field period of the survey. Like all respondents, the judges in this second wave received a follow-up email if they did not complete the survey; we sent the follow-up email on March 31, 2015. Thus, the first wave of judges received an invitation and two reminders, while the second wave received the follow up and one reminder. This error did not substantially affect the overall response rate of judges, as shown below.

4. A small number of respondents, either by preference or because of technical problems, requested to complete the survey on paper. For those submitting paper responses, FJC staff electronically entered their answers to all survey questions after the survey period ended.

5. While survey responses might be weighted in such circumstances, the results reported below are the unweighted survey responses. We did not weight survey responses for two reasons. First, we did not sample any of the respondent groups; we surveyed populations. Without a sampling frame, there is nothing by which to weight survey responses—except for probability of responding. We cannot weight by the probability of responding for a second reason: the respondent groups are not the same. Chief district judges and district judges responded as individuals. All other respondent groups were responding for an entire office, representing an unknown number of respondents. Because we do not know how many people each response represents, we cannot weight the responses as such. For these reasons, and given that we report only the frequencies with which responses occurred, it is not problematic to report unweighted survey results.

Table 1. Survey Response Rate

Respondents	Questionnaires Sent	Questionnaires Completed	Response Rate
Chief District Judges	94	77	82%
District Judges	929	611	66%
U.S. Attorney's Offices	93	62	66%
Federal Defenders and CJA District Panel Representative's Offices	178	128	72%
Chief Probation and Pretrial Services Offices	113	110	97%
Total	1,407	988	70%

A second issue of survey administration affected the responses of judges more than the other groups, though its impact was minimal. The list of district judges participating in the survey included active and senior status judges. Some senior status judges are in inactive status, while others are in active status, but no longer hear criminal cases as a matter of preference. Additionally, judges newly appointed to the bench may not have criminal cases on their docket, especially if they served in the U.S. Attorney's Office prior to their appointment. Thus, there are two groups of judges—those very new to the bench and those very senior—for whom a survey of harm to cooperators in criminal cases did not apply. To include the responses of these individuals would bias the number of instances of harm reported toward zero (they know of no instances of harm, but that is because they have no criminal cases). While, ideally, we would have excluded these judges from the survey population at the outset, such information was not systematically available on all judges, and we were not able to do so. After receiving the survey invitation, a number of judges contacted the FJC regarding their experience with criminal cases, either because they were new to the bench or they were in senior status (inactive or active but not taking criminal cases). We gave judges who contacted the FJC the option to complete the survey if they chose.[6] We closed the surveys of judges who opted against completing the survey for these reasons and removed them from the reported results. These exclusions bring the total response rate for district judges to 599 completed surveys out of a possible 899 district judges, or 67% of potential respondents. Table 2 shows the final response rates, after excluding those judges who notified us they were ineligible to answer the questionnaire.

---

6. A small number of additional judges were unable to complete the survey during the allotted time for other reasons, including poor health and international travel. We also removed these judges from the survey results reported below. Undoubtedly, more newly appointed and senior status judges could have been excluded from the survey totals. If the judges did not contact the FJC, however, there is no way for us to know this information.

Table 2. Revised Survey Response Rate

Respondents	Questionnaires Sent	Questionnaires Completed	Response Rate
Chief District Judges	94	77	82%
District Judges	899	599	67%
U.S. Attorney's Offices	93	62	66%
Federal Defenders and CJA District Panel Representative's Offices	178	128	72%
Chief Probation and Pretrial Services Offices	113	110	97%
Total	**1,377**	**976**	**71%**

We addressed a third issue of survey administration, related to the first, after closing the survey on April 8, 2015. For some survey respondents (but only in groups coordinating an office response) duplicate answers appeared in the data. Typically duplicates occurred because a respondent began answering the survey and then thought a designee, such as the criminal division chief in a district office of the U.S. attorneys, would be better suited to answer the questions. In all instances of duplicate answers, respondents notified the FJC of the issue and asked for a second survey link to be emailed to the designee. We compared the two responses to ensure no loss of data occurred with the removal of duplicate (partial) answers. One response, whether for an individual or office, remains in the data.

Despite these three issues, we find the survey results to be robust and reliable. Given the difficult nature of recalling the detailed events of the last three years, the limited timeframe for completing the survey, and the required efforts to coordinate a single office-wide response for the non-judge groups, a 71% response rate is high. Undoubtedly, the advance efforts to alert recipients to the survey, the follow-up reminders, and the salience of the topic contributed to so many people completing the survey. The high response rate increases our confidence in the results of the survey, reported below.

The geographic distribution of the survey responses further increases our confidence in the results. At least one judge from each of the 94 judicial districts responded to the survey, and 61% of the districts had responses from all groups. Defender and panel representative's offices responded from 83 different districts. The responses of probation and pretrial services offices represent the experiences of 92 different judicial districts. U.S. Attorney's Office responses were distributed across 62 judicial districts. Overall, we are confident the responses to the survey represent the national picture.

We should note one final issue affecting the reporting of the survey responses. Judges, defenders, prosecutors, probation officers, and pretrial services officers all see the same defendants/offenders and witnesses at different times. The instances of harm reported below undoubtedly include responses that detail the events in the same case from the perspectives of the judge, the attorneys, and the probation officers. Totaling the instances of harm across these groups risks over-counting the same event multiple times. Because we have no way of knowing if all groups are reporting the same events from different perspectives, we cannot remove any duplicate reporting of events. Instead, the results below report the range in instances of harm.

Analysis of Results

The first question on the survey asked respondents to report whether they knew of an instance in the past three years of harm or threat to defendants/offenders or witnesses (or their friends or family) because of the defendant/offender's or witness's cooperation with the government. If the respondent answered yes, we asked additional questions about the details of the harm or threat (described below). After the respondent answered the detailed questions on the first case, the initial screening question, followed by the detailed questions, repeated for up to five cases.

The results in Figure 1 show the percentage of respondents in each group reporting harm on each of up to five cases. The percentages reported for cases two through five were calculated for the subgroup that reported harm in the prior case. Ninety-seven percent of the 62 responding U.S. Attorney's Offices reported harm in a first case, while 49% of the 599 responding judges, 68% of defender offices, and 73% of probation offices reported a first case with harm.[7] Of the U.S. Attorney's Offices reporting harm in a first case, 95% reported harm in a second case as well. Overall, as a percentage of respondents, U.S. Attorney's Offices reported harm with greater frequency than any other group. In fact, more than 50% of U.S. Attorneys Offices responding to the survey reported harm in all five cases. Only 3% of U.S. Attorney's Offices reported no instances of harm or threat, whereas 27% of probation offices, 32% of defender offices, and 51% of the judges reported no instances of harm or threat.

---

7. Twenty-nine of the judges reporting no instances of harm stated later in the survey that they knew of no instances of harm because they were very new to the bench or in senior status and no longer hearing criminal cases. If we removed these judges from the total, as we did with the judges who alerted us to their status prior to completing the survey, the percentage of judges reporting on a first case of harm would be just over 50%.

Figure 1. Frequency of Harm or Threat Reported, by Respondent Group[8]

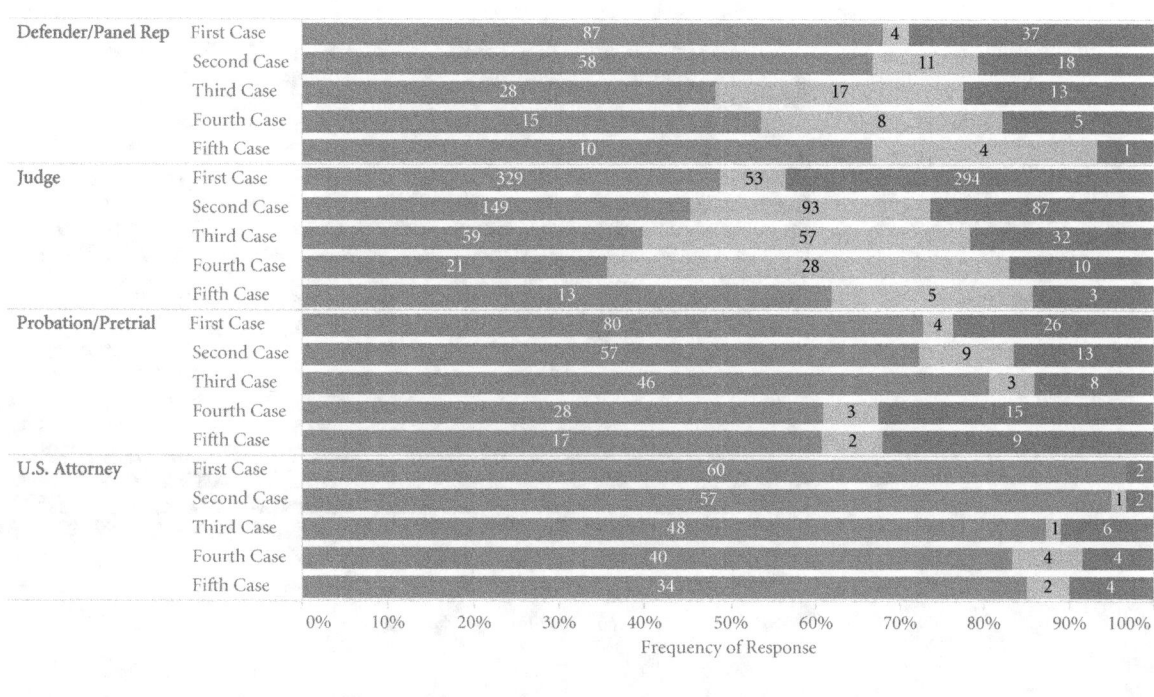

After reporting an instance of harm, respondents then described whether the harm or threat was directed at defendants/offenders or witnesses (or their family or friends). A respondent could choose both defendants/offenders and witnesses, if both were involved in the same case. Figure 2 shows the frequency with which defendants/offenders and witnesses were the subject of harm across all reported incidents. Respondents often reported harm to both defendants/offenders and witnesses in the same case.

---

8. Figures in this report, including Figure 1, show the frequency of an event by respondent groups, both as a percentage of the group and a number of reported events. The bars in Figure 1 show the frequency of harm as a percentage of the group, while the number on the bar is the actual number of instances of harm reported. For purposes of reporting, chief district judges and district judges are combined into a single group for all tables with one exception: Table 10, which reports district steps to protect cooperation information, includes the responses of chief district judges only, as they were the only group to receive that question.

Figure 2. Frequency of Harm or Threat to Defendants and Witnesses, by Respondent Group

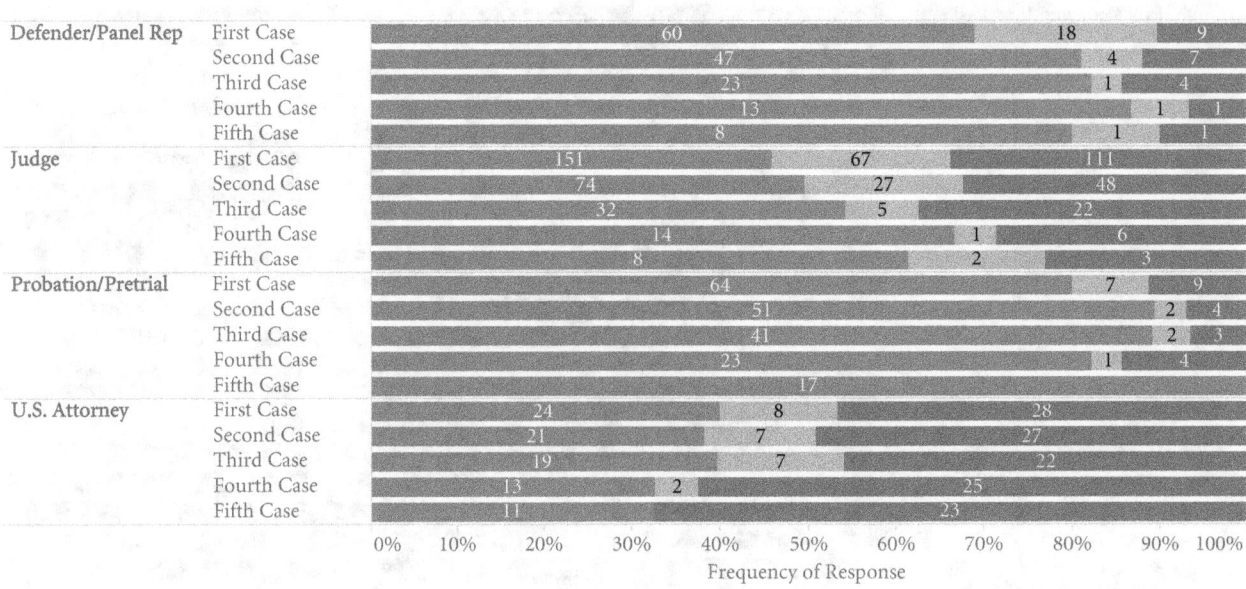

Taking these facts together, the results of the survey show that the 976 questionnaire respondents reported at least 571 instances of harm or threat to as many as 381 defendants/offenders and 292 witnesses in the past three years. These numbers, which are those reported by the judicial respondents, are the minimum number of instances of harm or threat. We assume that some number of instances reported by the other three groups of respondents are not duplicates of the instances reported by the judges and thus the actual incidence of harm and threat is higher.

Both the frequency of occurrence and the number of people harmed or threatened in the past three years are sufficient to provide details about the nature of threats and harm (reported below). While respondents did not always have complete information on the events that occurred, they provided a substantial amount of detailed information on the type of harm, the location of the individual at the time harm occurred, and the source for identifying cooperators. We report summaries of the details for defendants/offenders and witnesses separately below. The results are aggregated across all cases, though we would expect that the details of the first case are somewhat more cognitively available to the respondent (as it is the first case occurring to them) than the details of the fifth case. Of course, availability bias is more likely to be a problem for individual judicial respondents than other groups who provided an office response.

Harm or Threat to Defendants/Offenders

When respondents reported an instance of harm or threat to a defendant/offender, we asked them to detail the type of harm or threat that occurred. These details included the type of harm or threat, the location of the defendant/offender at the time of harm or threat, and the source used to identify the defendant/offender as a cooperator.

Types of harm or threat to defendants/offenders

Respondents could select as many categories as described the case in question.[9] If, for example, a defendant/offender was threatened with physical harm and then beaten, the respondent could check the boxes for both threats of physical harm and actual physical harm. Figure 3 reports all threats and harm to defendants/offenders reported by all respondent groups for all instances in the past three years. While the bar represents the frequency of the answer as a percentage of the group, the number on the bar is the actual number of responses in that category. Respondents most often reported threats of physical harm to the defendant/offender and to the friends and family of the defendant/offender. Over 80% of the incidents reported involved threats of physical harm, a minimum number of 339 instances. The minimum number of instances of actual harm (murder and other physical harm) is 133.

Those selecting the "Other" category detailed a variety of types of harm to the defendant.[10] While some of the incidents could be classified into the existing categories, two additional categories emerged from the "Other" responses: Internet/community/general threats and property damage. Internet/community/general threats included responses such as "told family members to put his name on rats.com," "flyers posted in his neighborhood," "[d]efendant's status as a cooperator was put on the internet," and "[n]ame posted on Top Snitches Facebook page." Property damage included shooting at the cars or houses of defendants, or harm to pets. We report the remaining details, which are too varied to categorize, in Appendix B.

Table 3. Categories of "Other" Harm or Threat to Defendants Specified by Respondents

Category of "Other" Harm or Threat	Number of Responses
Internet/Community/General Threats	16
Existing Categories	9
Property Damage	9
Other	5

9. It is for this reason that the types of harm or threat reported are higher than the number of defendants harmed or threatened.

10. When the questionnaire gave respondents the option to choose "Other," respondents were asked to specify what they meant. For every question where respondents could select "Other," we found instances of respondents selecting other without specifying what they meant, or writing in a specification without having chosen "Other." To prevent loss of information, the Appendices report all specified comments, regardless of whether "Other" was selected as a category or not. For each of the "Other" options, we made an initial attempt to categorize these comments. We report this categorization in the tables in the text, while the items coded into each category can be found in the Appendices. All specifications and open-ended responses reported in the Appendices were lightly edited for clarity and redacted to prevent identifying either the case or the respondent.

Figure 3. Frequency of the Type of Harm or Threat Directed at Defendants, by Respondent Group

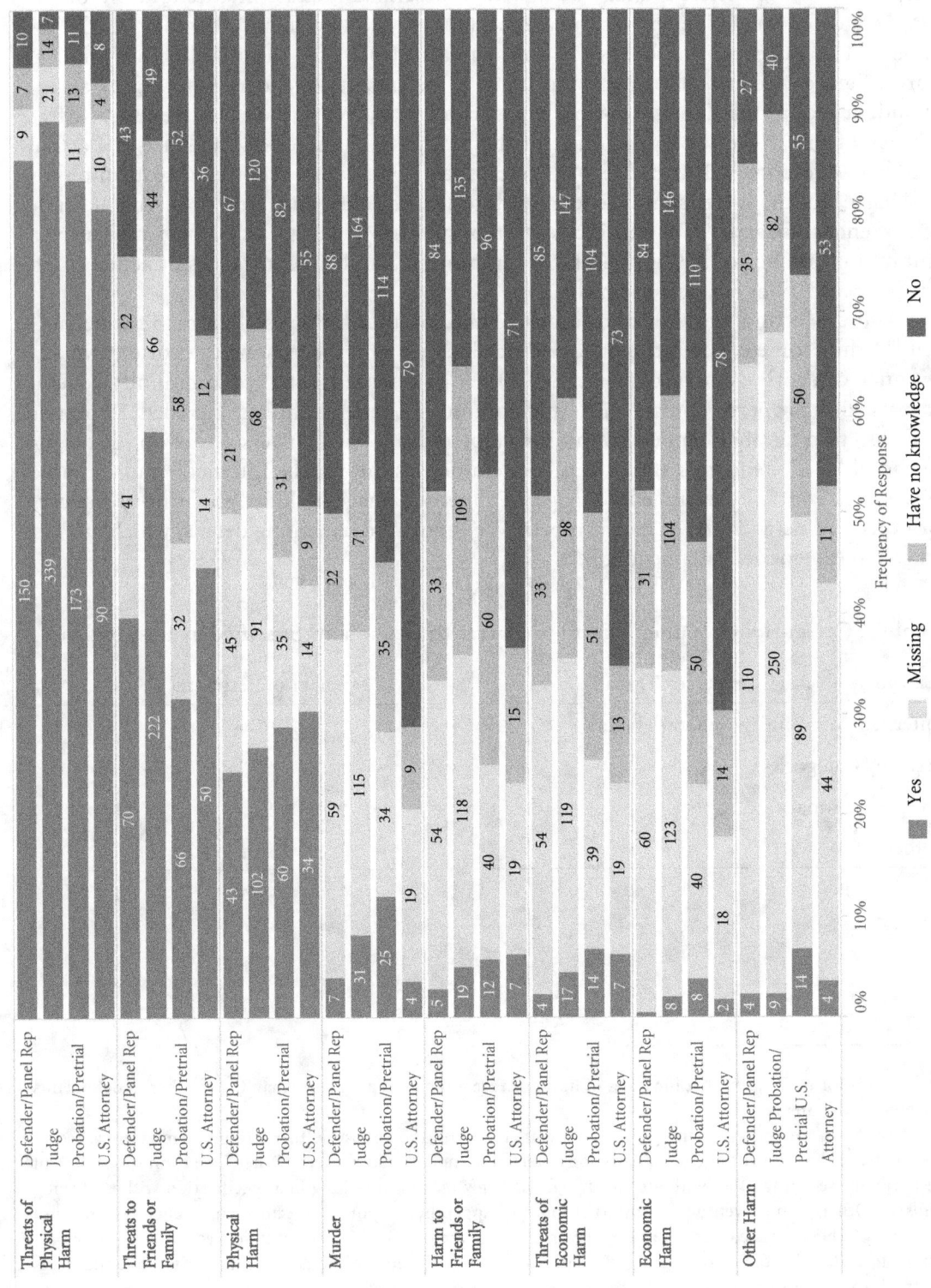

Location of the defendant/offender at the time of harm or threat

After reporting the details of harm or threat, respondents identified the location of the defendant/offender at the time the harm or threat occurred. Once again, because respondents reported multiple instances of harm or threat for each case, more than one location could be chosen. Figure 4 reports the number and percentage of respondents reporting each location across all respondents and all cases. Respondents most often reported that defendants/offenders were harmed or threatened while in pretrial detention—a minimum of 207 instances—followed by pretrial release and incarceration—a minimum of 125 instances. Chief probation and pretrial services offices reported the location of the defendant/offender as "on probation" more often than other groups, which is not surprising given their contact with defendants/offenders at that time. Overall, as a percentage, respondents reported a substantial amount of harm occurring while defendants were in custody of some kind.

Figure 4. Frequency of Reported Location of Defendant at the Time of Harm or Threat, by Respondent Group

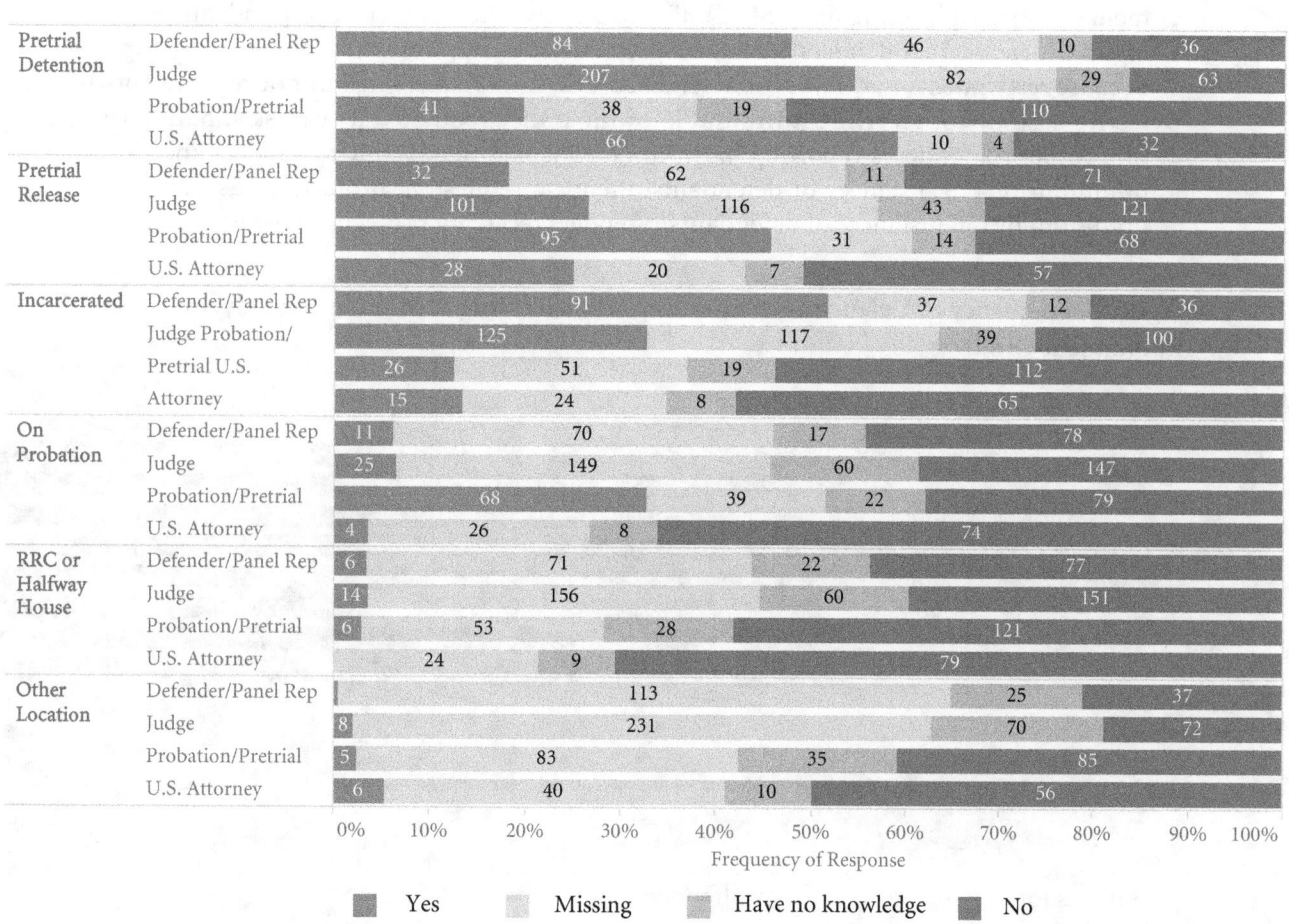

Respondents also specified "Other" locations for the defendant/offender at the time of harm or threat. The "Other" response provided most often was that the defendant/offender was not in any form of custody. The second most common response included defendants/offenders who were in some other form of custody that we did not specify. We report other specified options provided by respondents in Appendix C.

Table 4. Categories of "Other" Defendant Locations Specified by Respondents

Category of "Other" Locations	Number of Responses
Not in Custody of Any Kind	13
Other Forms of Custody	10
Other	7

Protective custody

One set of questions, only for those reporting harm to defendants/offenders, asked respondents if the defendant/offender requested or received protective custody or placement in a special housing unit (SHU). Figure 5 shows the number of respondents reporting that defendants/offenders requested protective custody and the number receiving it. Because respondents may know of defendants/offenders requesting but not receiving protective custody (or receiving it without knowing if they requested it) we asked both questions of all respondents reporting harm to defendants/offenders. Respondents knew of a minimum of 128 instances of defendants/offenders requesting protective custody and a minimum of 136 instances of defendants/offenders receiving protective custody.

Figure 5. Frequency of Defendants Requesting and Receiving Protective Custody, by Respondent Group

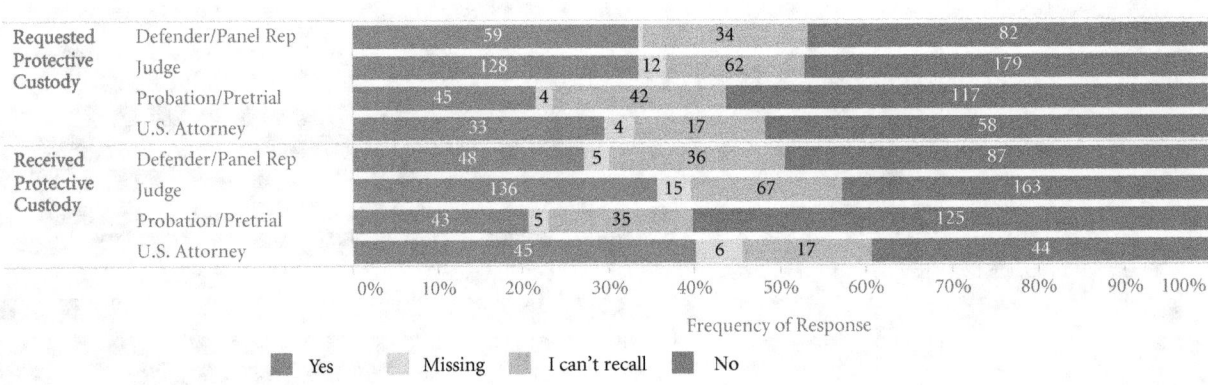

Sources for identifying defendants/offenders

We asked respondents to report any court documents used to identify the defendant/offender as a cooperator. Respondents could report multiple sources. Figure 6 shows the percentage and number of respondents reporting the use of each type of document for identifying the defendant/offender as a cooperator. The plea agreement or plea supplement was the document most frequently used to identify a defendant/offender as a cooperator—a minimum of 135 instances—with a 5K1.1 motion used nearly as often—a minimum of 111 instances.

Figure 6. Frequency of the Use of Court Documents to Identify Defendant Cooperators, by Respondent Group

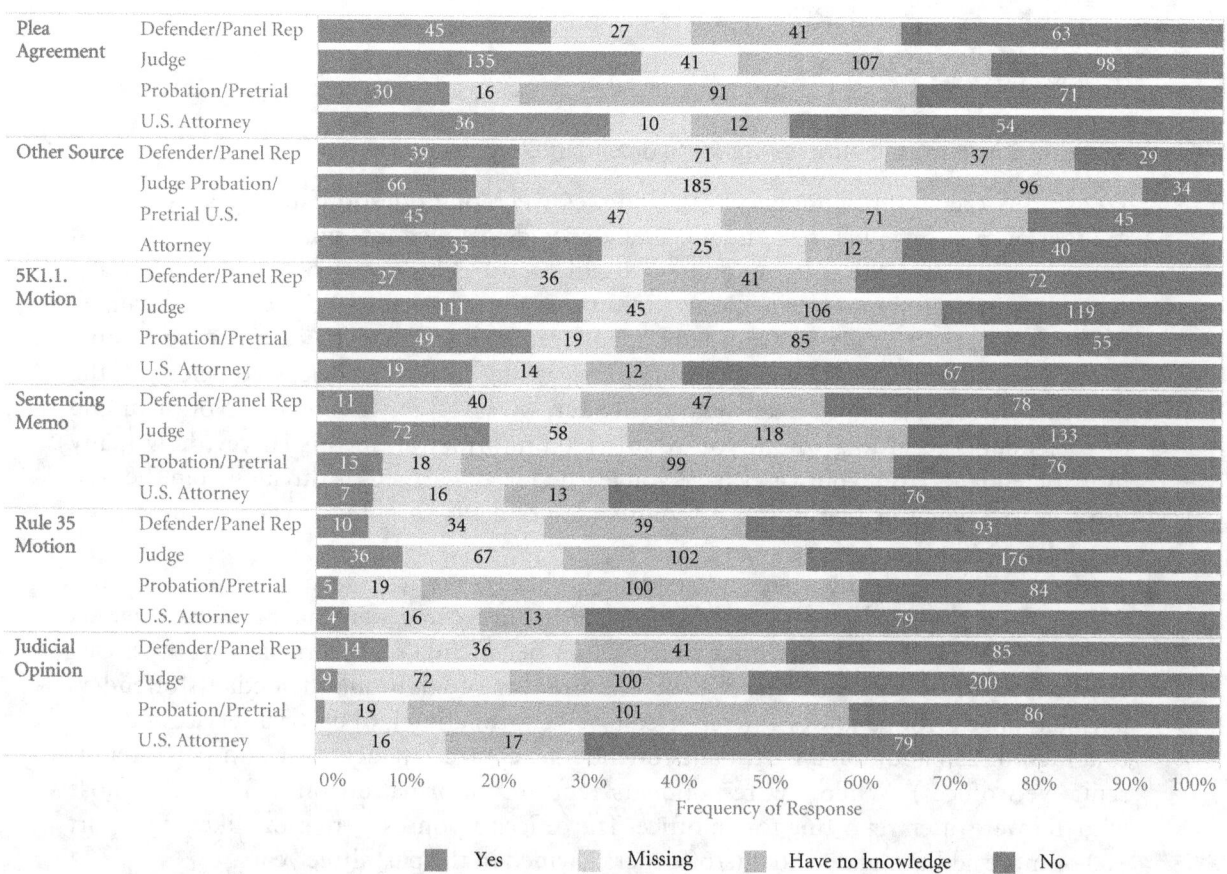

Regarding the "Other" sources by which cooperators were identified, a single category emerged. Respondents frequently reported use of other court documents or proceedings, especially discovery, testimony, and inferences from docket activity (such as sealed entries or gaps in docket sequence numbers) to identify defendant/offender cooperators. Appendix D details the exact sources of information while Table 5 shows the categorization of those details.

Table 5. Categories of "Other" Sources Used to Identify Defendant Cooperators Specified by Respondents

Categories of "Other" Sources	Number of Responses
Other Court Documents/Proceedings	165
Talking to Agents/Debriefing/Government Disclosure	14
Codefendant/Known	14
Suspicion	12
Other	11
News Reports	5

Additional instances of harm or threat to defendants/offenders

To avoid overtaxing respondents with an excessively long questionnaire, we capped the number of cases on which respondents could provide detailed information at five. We did not, however, want the total amount of harm reported by the survey to be artificially capped by this number. To provide an indication of how much additional harm occurred in the past three years, we asked respondents reporting on a fifth case two additional questions, one regarding defendants and one regarding witnesses (discussed below). If the fifth case involved harm to a defendant/offender, we asked the following: "Not including the defendants regarding whom you've provided information in this survey, how many more defendants from your cases have you learned were harmed or threatened in the past three years?" For this question, we required respondents to enter a whole number, between 0 and 100.[11]

Figure 7 shows the number of defendants/offenders reported by all groups. If we sum the numbers provided by all respondents, and assume there were no duplicate answers across groups, we find a maximum of 579 more defendants/offenders harmed or threatened with harm in the past three years. The number of additional defendants/offenders harmed ranged from a low of 21 (reported by chief probation and pretrial services offices) to a high of 236 additional defendants/offenders (reported by defender and panel representative's offices). While few respondents reported information on a fifth case, those who did were often reporting for an office. The office responses were more likely to report 100 or more additional defendants/offenders harmed in the past three years.

---

11. Initial discussions within the FJC and with AO staff suggested that capping this number at 100 would yield more reliable data. A handful of respondents found this cap to be a source of frustration and chose to report their frustration, as well as a number over 100, in their open-ended responses (see below).

Figure 7. Frequency of Additional Instances of Harm or Threat to Defendants, by Respondent Group

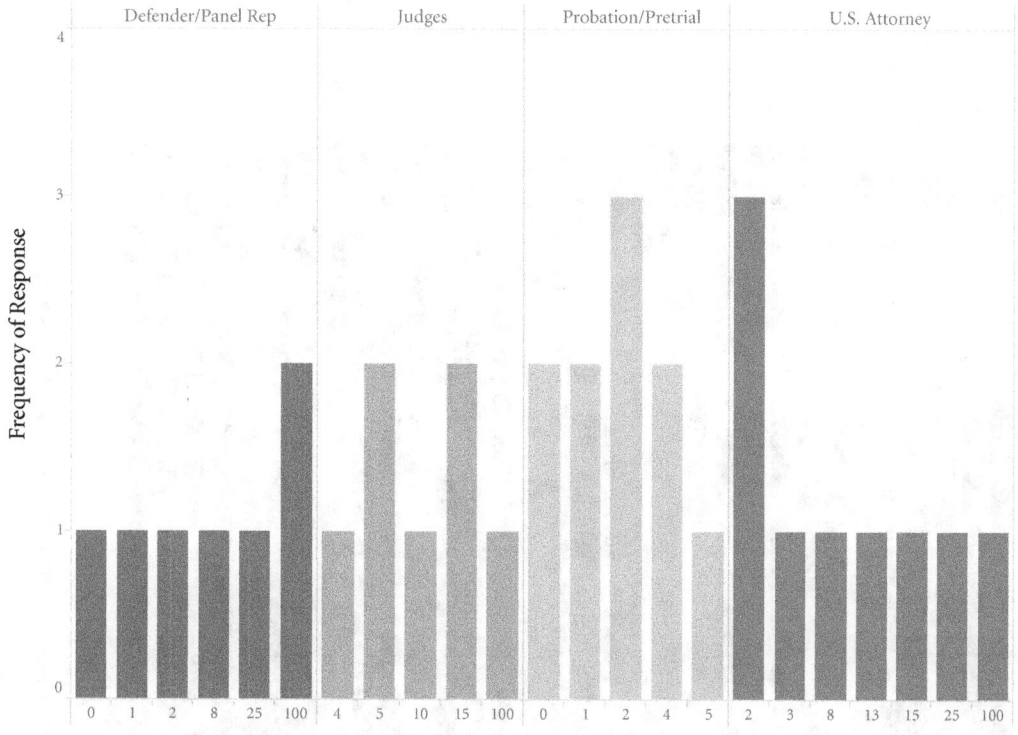

Number of Additional Defendants Reported Harmed

Summary of results on harm or threat to defendants/offenders

To summarize the findings regarding harm to defendants/offenders, respondents reported a minimum of 381 instances of harm or threat directed at defendants/offenders for their cooperation (or perceived cooperation) with the federal government over the past three years (Figure 2). A minimum of an additional 236 defendants/offenders experienced harm or threat, though we have no additional information on the circumstances of these events (Figure 7). When the harm or threat occurred, the defendant/offender was in some form of custody, including pretrial detention or incarceration. In many instances defendants/offenders were identified as cooperators by use of court documents, especially plea agreements or plea supplements, 5K1.1 motions, and docketing activity such as the presence of sealed entries and gaps in docket sequence numbers (Figure 6 and Table 5).

Harm or Threat to Witnesses

In addition to reporting information on the harm to defendants/offenders for cooperating with the government, the survey asked respondents to report on harm to witnesses. While the questions are largely the same as those for defendant/offender cooperators, the results are somewhat different. Overall, detailed information on harm to witnesses appears to be less readily available to respondents. Nonetheless, there is still sufficient information for examination.

Figure 8. Frequency of the Type of Harm or Threat Directed at Witnesses, by Respondent Group

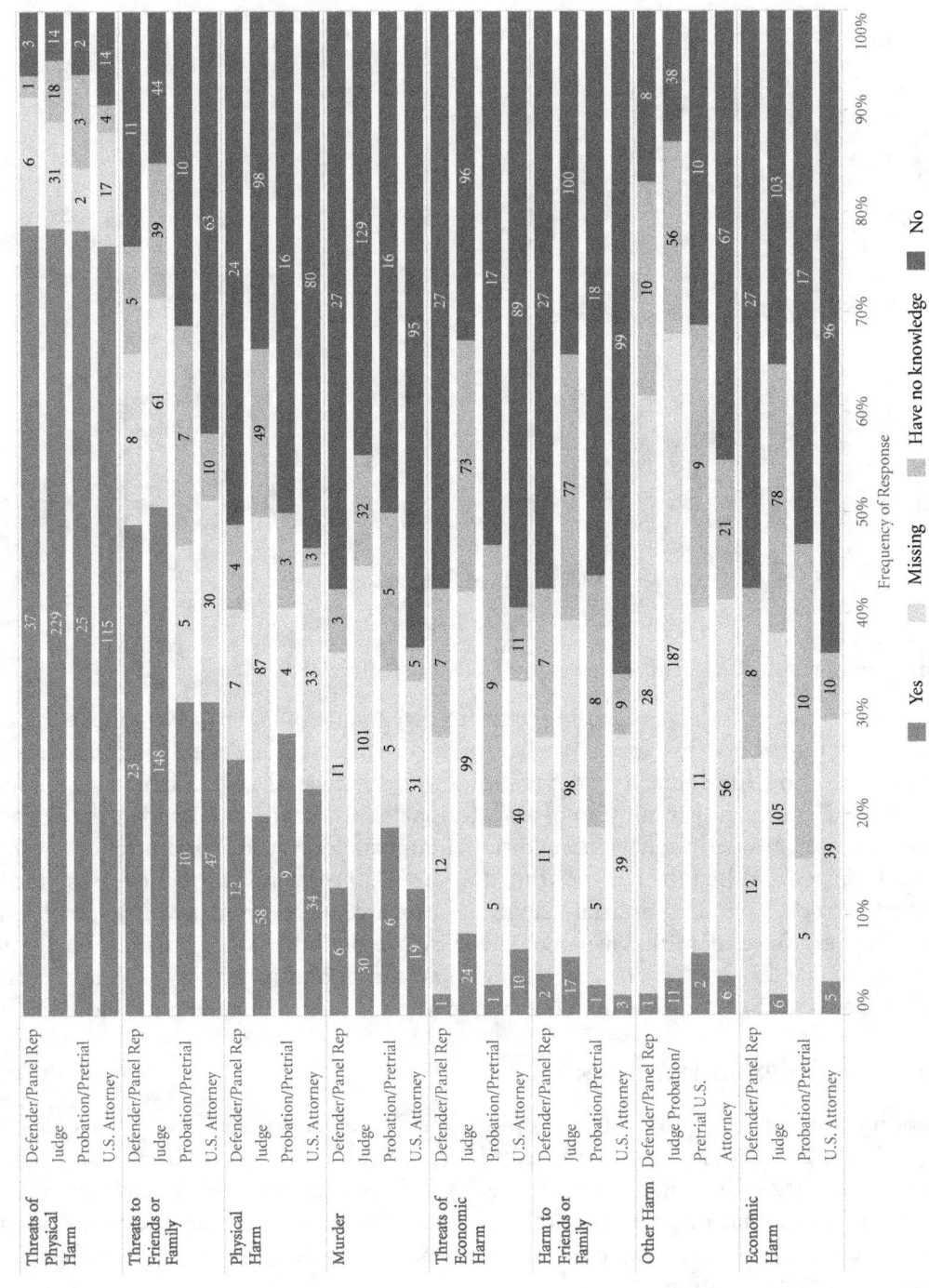

Types of harm or threat to witnesses

Figure 8 reports the types of harm or threat directed at witnesses thought to be cooperating with the government. Similar to defendants/offenders, the most common types of harm are threats of physical harm, threats to friends and family, and actual physical harm. At minimum, in the three-year period, respondents reported 229 instances where a witness was threatened with physical harm, 148 instances involved threats to a friend or family member, and 88 instances involving actual physical harm (murder or physical harm other than murder). Because some of the instances reported by defender, probation, and U.S. Attorney's Offices are almost certainly not duplicates of the instances reported by judges, the actual number of instances of harm or threat of harm to witnesses was likely higher.

Relatively few respondents chose "Other" as the type of harm or threat directed at witnesses. We report the details of these other types of harm in Appendix E, including attempted murder, contracting to kill a witness, general threats and harassment, and property damage. Table 6 shows the categorization of the "Other" categories.

Table 6. Categories of "Other" Harm or Threat to Witnesses Specified by Respondents

"Other" Categories of Harm or Threat	Number of Responses
Other	15
Internet/Community/General Threats	8
Property Damage	4
Attempted Murder	3
Existing Categories	2

Location of witnesses at the time of harm or threat

Figure 9 shows the reported location of witnesses at the time the harm or threat occurred. Here we see a number of differences from the locations listed for the defendants. Witnesses were likely to be in pretrial detention (often because they are uncharged coconspirators or codefendants—as reported in the open-ended comments) or on pretrial release. At a minimum, 85 incidents occurred when the witness was in pretrial detention and 63 instances occurred when the witness was on pretrial release. The next most common locations for witnesses were "Other"—a minimum of 55 instances—and incarceration—a minimum of 49 instances. As Table 7 shows, the "Other" location for witnesses was almost always not in custody—i.e., they were at home, at work, or in their community—because they were uncharged. We report the complete list of locations in Appendix F. We should note that many respondents were unable to report the location of witnesses at the time the harm or threat occurred.

Figure 9. Frequency of Reported Location of Witness at the Time of Harm or Threat, by Respondent Group

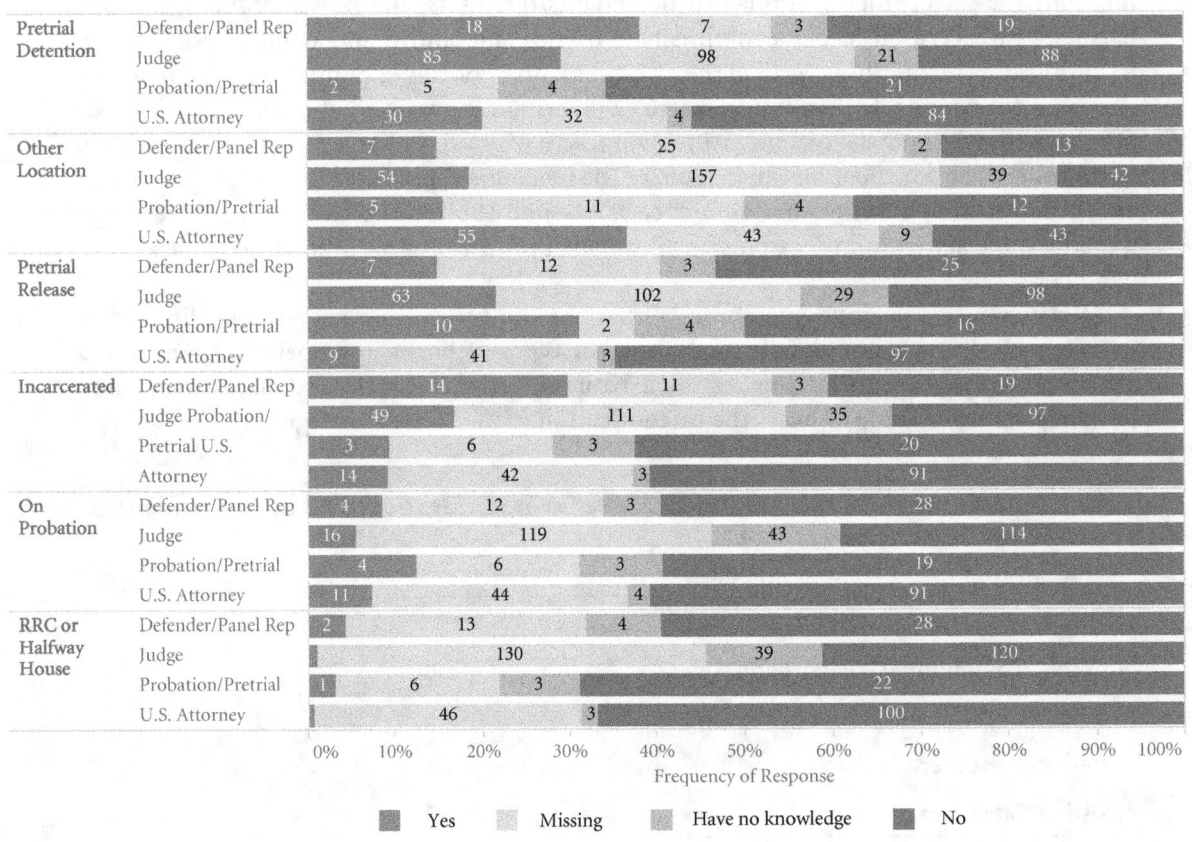

Table 7. Categories of "Other" Witness Locations Specified by Respondents

Categories of "Other" Locations	Number of Responses
Not in Custody of Any Kind	130
Other	21
Existing Category	4

Sources for identifying witnesses

The sources for identifying a cooperating witness also show a different pattern than we reported for the defendants/offenders. While respondents reported that cooperating defendants/offenders were identified in 5K1.1 motions or plea agreements, witness identification occurred most often through "Other" sources, discussed in more detail below. Figure 10 reports the sources used to identify cooperating witnesses and shows that at a minimum witnesses were identified through "Other" sources 59 times. Plea agreements or plea supplements were used to identify cooperating witnesses in 54 instances.

Figure 10. Frequency of the Use of Court Documents to Identify Witness Cooperators, by Respondent Group

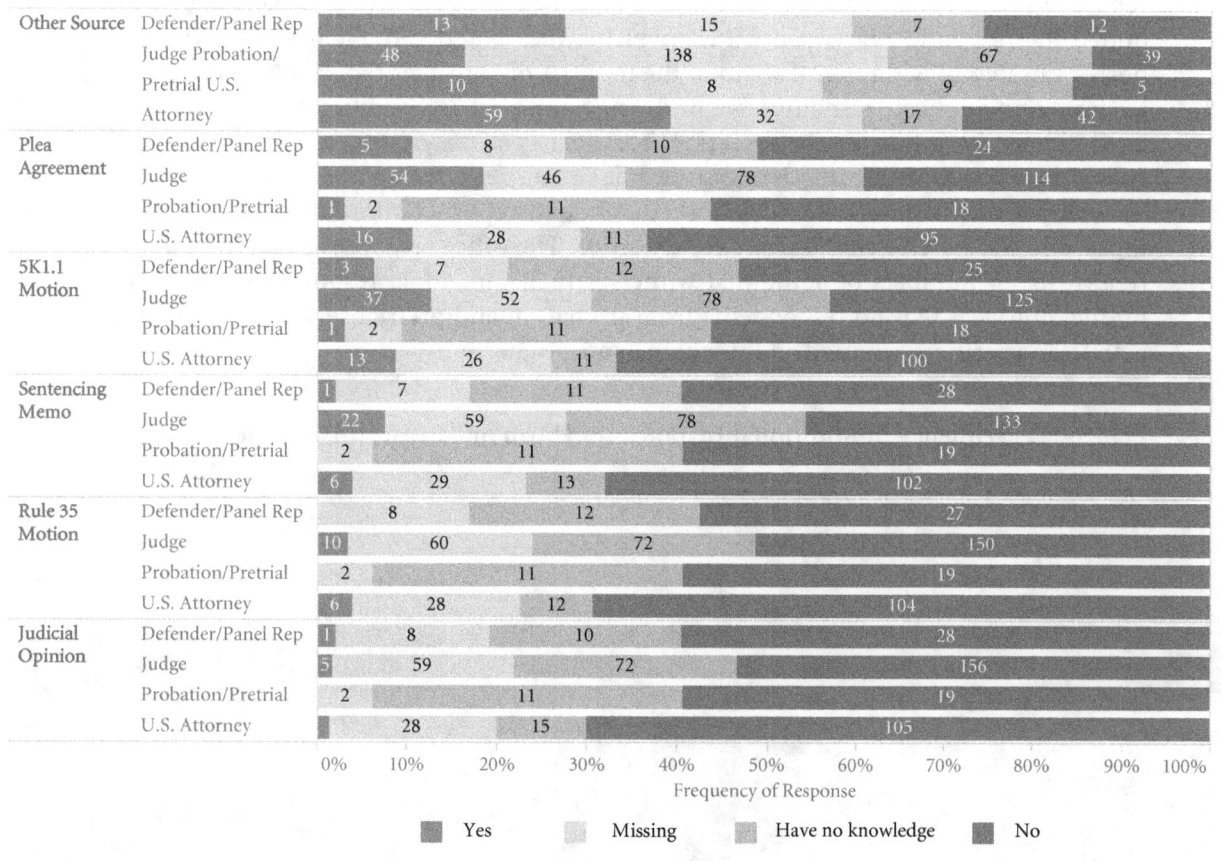

Similar to defendants/offenders, respondents often reported witnesses being identified through other court documents, especially testimony, witness lists, and during discovery. Table 8 reports the categorization of the specified responses, which are provided in Appendix G.

Table 8. Categories of "Other" Sources Used to Identify Witness Cooperators Specified by Respondents

Categories of "Other" Sources	Number of Responses
Other Court Documents/Proceedings	135
Codefendants/Known	15
Other	12
Suspicion	7
Talking to Agents/Debriefs/Government Disclosure	2
News	1

Additional instances of harm or threat to witnesses

We asked respondents reporting information about a fifth case of harm to witnesses to report any additional harm to witnesses from the past three years. Once again, we required the respondents to choose a number between 0 and 100. Figure 11 shows the reported number of witnesses. If we total the number of witnesses reportedly harmed, again assuming no duplicate responses, we find a maximum of 365 additional witnesses threatened or harmed in the past three years. U.S. Attorney's Offices reported an additional 301 instances of harm or threat to witnesses, while judges reported an additional 64 instances. As with defendants/offenders, while few respondents reported information on a fifth case, those who did were often reporting for an office. The office responses were more likely to report higher numbers of additional witnesses than individual respondents. It is worth noting, however, that no respondents from probation and pretrial services offices or federal defender offices reported additional instances of harm.

Figure 11. Frequency of Additional Instances of Harm or Threat to Witnesses

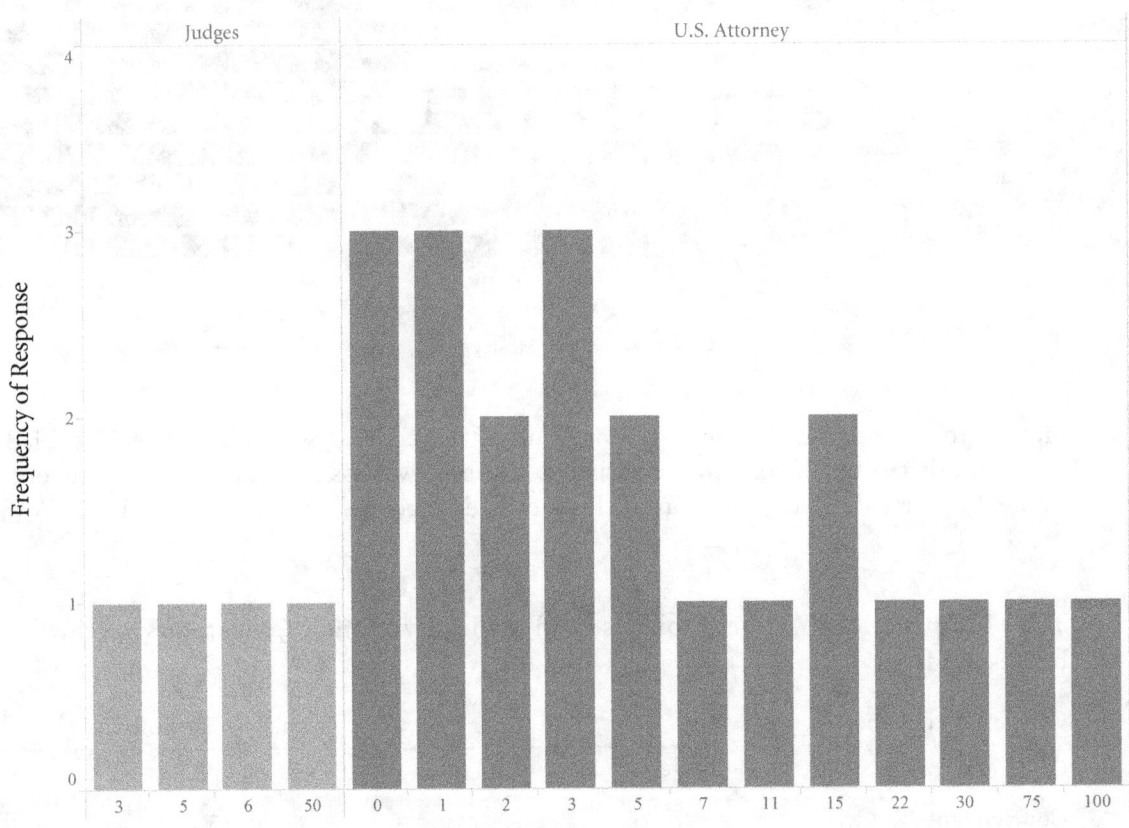

Summary of results on harm or threat to witnesses

While respondents reported harm to witnesses less frequently than they reported harm to defendants/offenders, a minimum of 292 instances of harm or threat to witnesses occurred in the past three years (Figure 8). An additional 301 instances of harm or threat occurred, but we cannot report the details of these additional events (Figure 11). Witnesses were more likely than defendants/offenders to be out of custody at the time they were harmed, though many were also in custody as codefendants or uncharged coconspirators (Figure 9). Identification of witnesses often occurred through court documents, specifically witness lists, through testimony, and during discovery (Figure 10).

Additional Questions

In addition to questions about the frequency of harm to defendants/offenders and witnesses, the questionnaire included other items designed to shed light on harm to cooperators. We asked those questions only of the relevant respondent groups.

Defendant/offender requests for court documents or docket sealing

We asked federal defenders and CJA district panel representative's offices about the frequency with which their clients requested court documents to prove they were not a cooperator, and the frequency with which their clients asked them to seal all or part of the CM/ECF docket. For both questions, we asked respondents to enter a number between 0 and 100. The results in Figures 12 and 13 summarize the number of federal defenders and CJA district panel representatives who reported such requests, by number of defendant/offenders who made such requests. As the results demonstrate, many more defense attorneys report requests for court documents than requests to seal all or part of a CM/ECF docket. When we total the number of defendants/offenders requesting court documents, we find 1,941 requests, likely a low number given the frequency with which defense counsel reported "100 defendants" (the maximum permitted by the question format). Defense counsel also reported a total of 704 defendants/offenders requesting sealing all or part of their CM/ECF dockets.

Figure 12. Frequency of Requests for Court Documents

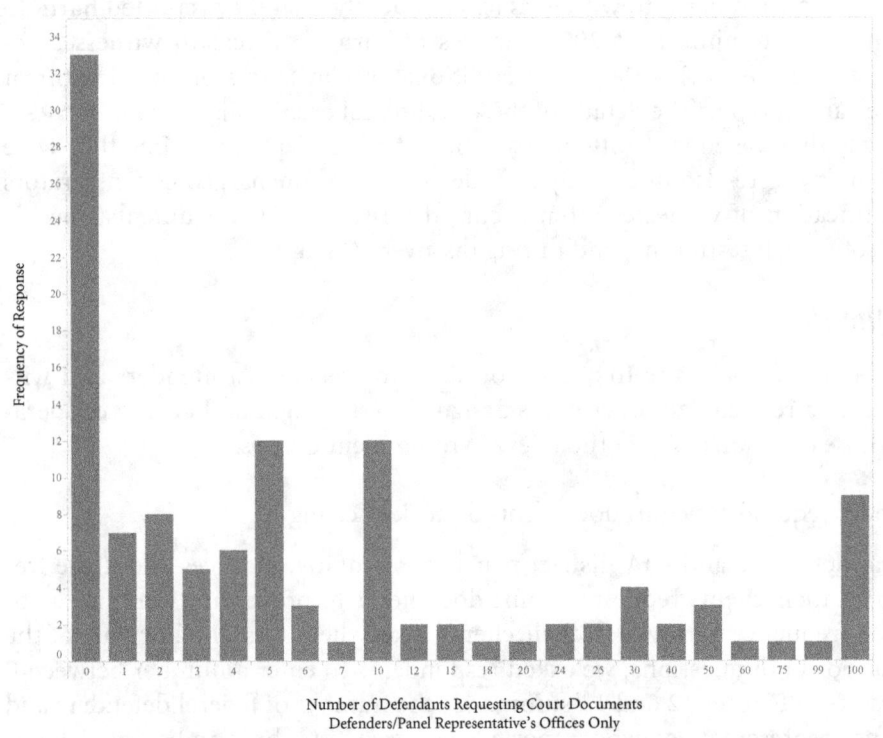

Number of Defendants Requesting Court Documents
Defenders/Panel Representative's Offices Only

Figure 13. Frequency of Request for Docketing Sealing

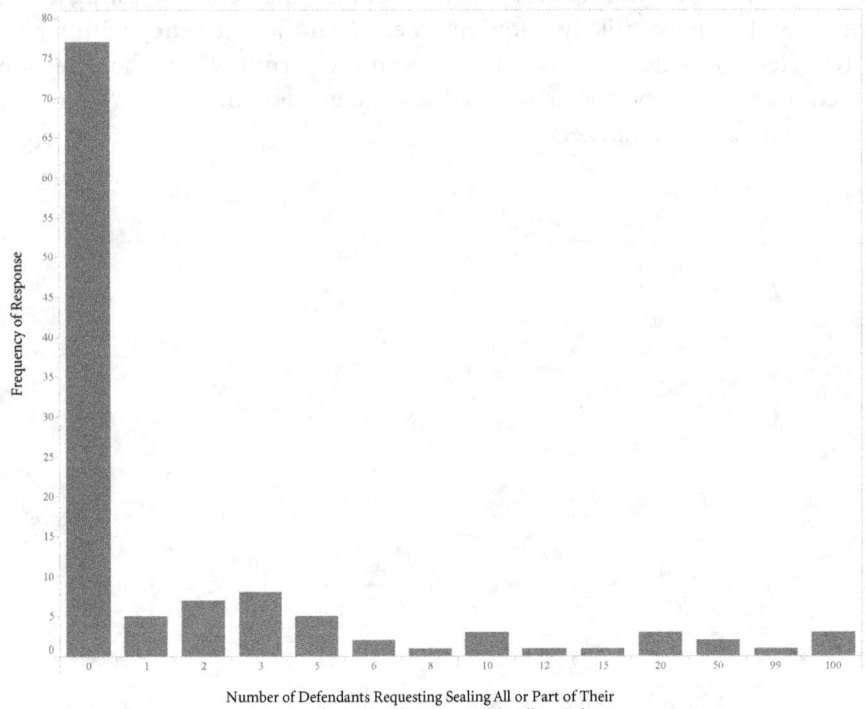

Number of Defendants Requesting Sealing All or Part of Their
Dockets Defenders/Panel Representative's Offices Only

Survey of Harm to Cooperators: Final Report • Federal Judicial Center • 2016

Withdrawing or refusing cooperation

Both defense and prosecuting attorneys answered two questions about the frequency with which, in the past three years, defendants/offenders and witnesses withdrew offers of cooperation, or refused cooperation, because of actual or threatened harm. Once again, we asked respondents to report a number between 0 and 100. Figures 14 and 15 report the number of respondents who reported defendant/offender withdrawal or refusal of cooperation, and Figures 16 and 17 report the same information for witnesses. The number of defendants/offenders withdrawing offers ranged from a low of 197 (reported by U.S. Attorney's Offices) to a high of 247 (reported by defenders and panel representative's offices). The number of defendants/offenders refusing cooperation ranged from a low of 527 (U.S. Attorney's Offices) to a high of 758 (defenders and panel representative's offices). Respondents reported the number of witnesses withdrawing offers of cooperation less often. U.S. Attorney's Offices reported 174 withdrawals while defender and panel representative's offices reported 192 instances of witnesses withdrawing offers of cooperation. Respondents reported witnesses refusing to cooperate more frequently than withdrawing offers. The number of witnesses refusing cooperation ranged from a low of 364 instances (defender and panel representative's offices) to a high of 467 instances (U.S. Attorney's Offices).

Figure 14. Frequency of Defendants Withdrawing Cooperation

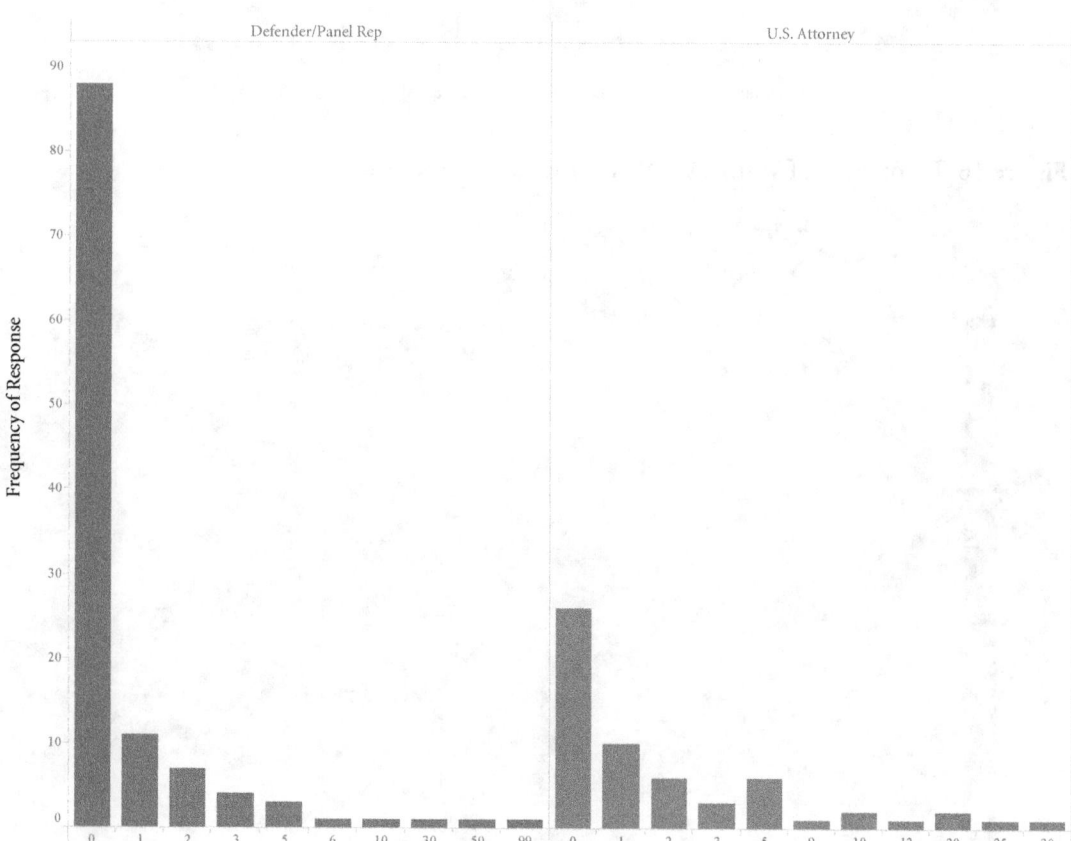

Number of Defendants Withdrawing Offers of Cooperation

Figure 15. Frequency of Defendants Refusing Cooperation

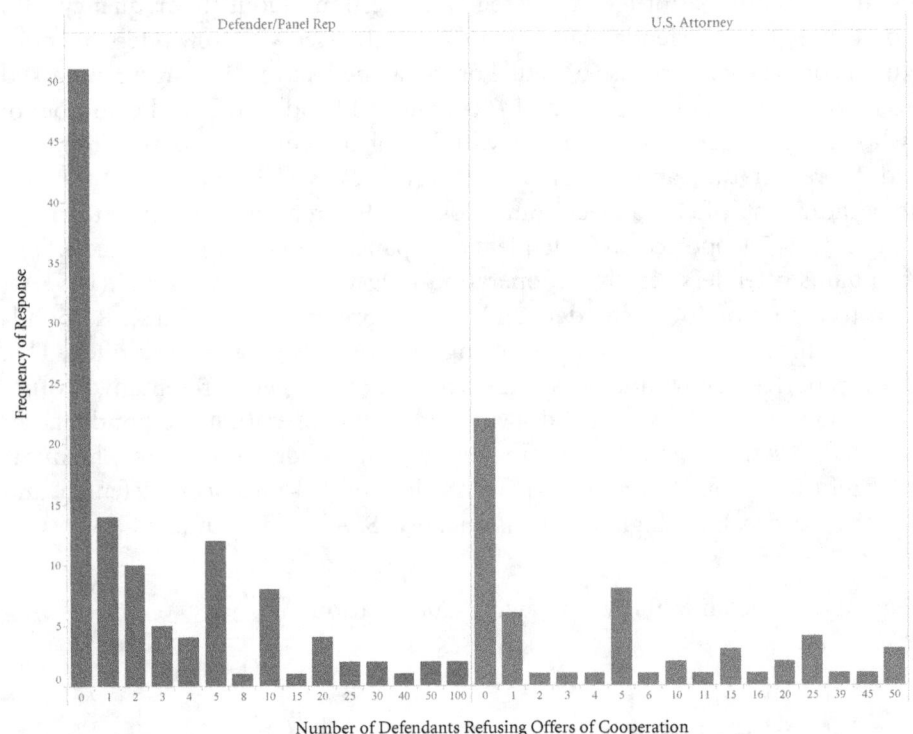

Number of Defendants Refusing Offers of Cooperation

Figure 16. Frequency of Witnesses Withdrawing Cooperation

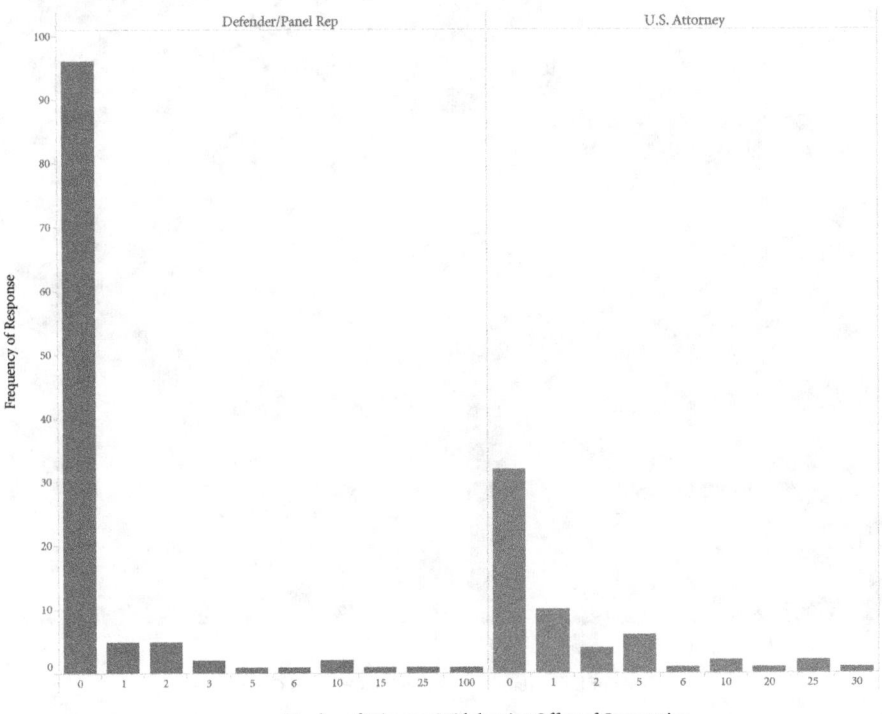

Number of Witnesses Withdrawing Offers of Cooperation

Figure 17. Frequency of Witnesses Refusing Cooperation

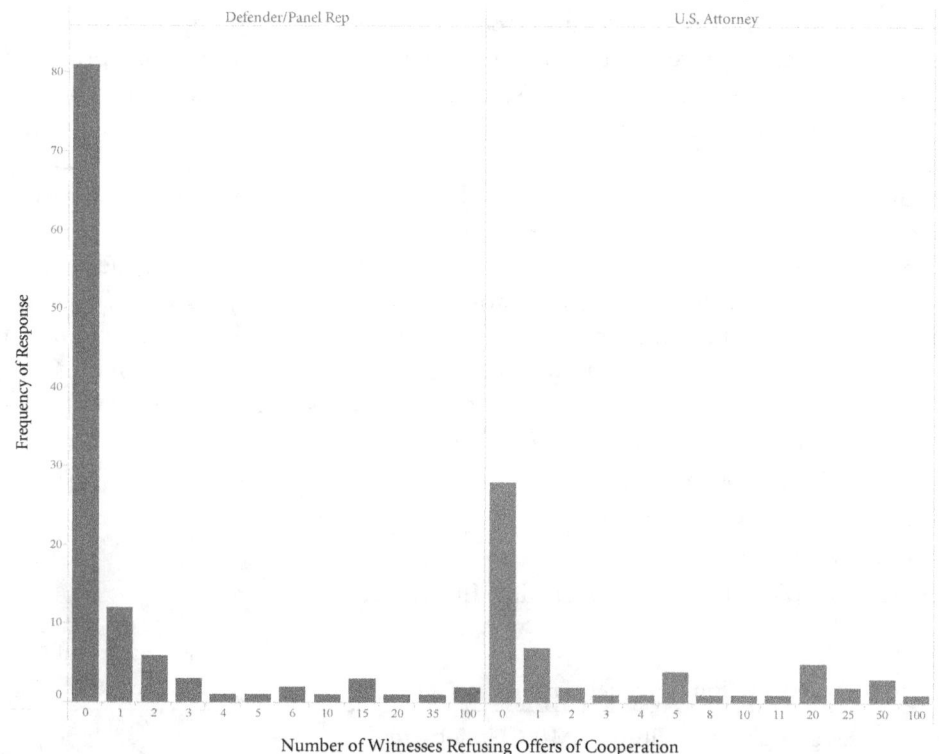

Comparing the frequency of harm or threat in 2014 to 2013

We asked all respondent groups to compare the frequency with which defend-ants/offenders and witnesses were harmed in 2014 compared to 2013. Table 9 reports the results, but they should be interpreted with caution. The vast majority of respondents, across all groups, were unable to provide a comparison, choosing "I don't know" over all other options. Of the substantive categories, respondents most often reported the frequency of harm being about the same in 2014 compared with 2013. Given that respond-ents clearly did not have trouble remembering instances of harm, or the details of such harm, their inability to compare two years is more likely the result of the wording of the question or the difficulty of the task (for a question at the end of the survey) than a lack of harm one year to the next. The results should be read with these caveats in mind.

Table 9. Comparing the Frequency of Harm or Threat, 2014 to 2013, by Group

Respondents	Higher in 2014	About the Same in 2014	Lower in 2014	I don't know/missing	Total
Judges	32	147	15	480	674
Defenders/Panel Representative's Offices	10	44	5	67	126
U.S. Attorney's Offices	14	32	3	13	62
Chief Probation and Pretrial Services Offices	11	32	8	58	109

District steps to protect cooperating information

One final question on the survey, asked only of chief district judges, attempted to uncover actions taken by districts to protect cooperator information. The list of options provided (shown below) allowed respondents to choose multiple items. Table 10 shows the frequency with which chief district judges reported their courts taking these steps. No one chose "none of the above" and relatively few chose to specify an "Other" option, suggesting the categories covered the majority of steps taken by districts to protect information about cooperators.

Clearly the most common action taken by the district courts has been, at the request of parties, to seal documents containing cooperation information; sixty-six of the seventy-seven chief district judges who completed the questionnaire said their district had taken this action. Nearly half of the respondents also reported that their district seals, *sua sponte*, documents containing cooperation information and/or makes criminal documents appear identically on CM/ECF to obscure cooperation information. The other specific actions are less frequently used, as shown in Table 10. (We report the specified "Other" options in Appendix H.)

Table 10. District Efforts to Protect Cooperation Information

Method of Protecting Cooperation Information	Frequency of Selection
Making criminal cases appear identically on CM/ECF to obscure cooperation information (such as requiring filing sealed supplements with a plea agreement)	33
Sealing documents containing cooperation information *sua sponte*	37
Sealing documents containing cooperation information at the request of the parties	66
Ordering parties to redact cooperation information from documents	19
Restricting remote access of documents containing cooperation information	29
Allowing public access of documents containing cooperation information only in the courthouse or clerk's office	9
Removing documents containing cooperation information from public files	19
Requiring the entry of documents containing cooperation to be private entries in CM/ECF	21
Other (please specify) _____	7
None of the above	0

Open-ended comments summary

At the end of the survey, respondents were offered an opportunity to provide additional comments. Over a third of all respondents chose to make additional comments, and they covered a wide range of topics. We read the content of these comments and found we could group them into twelve different categories. Comments that were especially lengthy or detailed were coded into multiple categories, with no comment falling into more than six categories. Table 11 below shows the frequency of comments in each category. For those categories where comments could take a negative tone, instead of the positive or affirmative tone implied by the category, the number of negative comments is reported below the main category heading.

Table 11. Open-Ended Comment Coding

Coding of Comments	Frequency
General comment about the frequency of harm	148
Harm is not frequent	15
General comments about the sources to identify cooperator	106
Court documents were not the source	4
Details about a specific incident	96
Nothing to report	85
Procedures for protecting defendants	81
General comment about harm in prison/prison culture	76
Takes issue with the survey[12]	33
Policy comments	29
Concerns about a national judiciary policy	7
Comments about refusal to cooperate out of fear	27
Refusals out of fear do not occur	1
Procedures to protect witnesses	15
"Missing"	2
Procedures for protecting juries	1

Some categories required no additional coding for tone or nuance. For example, if a respondent provided additional information about an already reported event, or chose to add information about additional instances of harm, the comment was coded into the category for "details about a specific incident." Likewise, when respondents reported spe-

---

12. While most of the survey comments reported more information about the scope of harm or the policy implications of harm or threat, some respondents used the open-ended comments to take issue with the use of a survey to determine the scope of the problem, or to complain about the upper bound on the number of people they could report. Overall, these comments could be categorized as suggesting that the harm occurring is more than they were able to report in the survey.

cific procedures for protecting defendants, juries, or witnesses, we coded the comment into those categories. The comments falling into the four categories of details about incidents, or procedures to protect defendants, witnesses, or juries, provided interesting information about what has happened in the past, and how districts have worked to overcome these problems. Typically the procedures to protect defendants or witnesses included sealing, either as a general principle or by local rule, or obscuring docket entries, including substituting revised plea agreements for the original, or discussing cooperation in a court proceeding rather than through written motions.

Other categories, however, required some additional clarification. Comments about the frequency of harm, for example, could either suggest that harm or threats were frequent or infrequent. Of the 148 comments about the frequency of threat or harm in the district, only 15 suggested that harm or threats were infrequent (eight judges, five defenders, one U.S. Attorney's Office, and one chief probation and pretrial services office). At times the respondents noted that harm was infrequent because of recent steps taken by the district to better protect cooperation information. Other times, respondents were noting that harm to a specific group, such as witnesses, was infrequent. Lastly, respondents also noted they did not have or were not likely to be told of such threats, so they thought such instances were infrequent. Of course, the 85 respondents who specifically said they had nothing to report, because they didn't have criminal cases, could be included with other respondents who said harm was infrequent based on their experience. Nonetheless, even after combining "nothing to report" with the 15 respondents who said harm was infrequent, the tone of the comments overall would still suggest respondents found harm to be frequent rather than infrequent.

The remaining 133 respondents who said harm was frequent used words such as "often," "every," "many," "most," "all," or "the vast majority," to describe how often cooperators were threatened, explicitly or implicitly, with harm or were victims of harm. Several of these respondents noted that the problems of threat and harm to cooperators are especially pronounced in drug and gang cases, as well as in certain geographic communities. Overall, when respondents were noting the frequency with which harm or threat occurred, they found it to be pervasive.

Comments about the sources used to identify cooperators typically provided information about which court documents were most likely to identify a cooperator, including those most frequently demanded in federal prisons when a new inmate joins a facility (discussed below). In fact, only 4 of 106 comments about sources used to identify cooperators explicitly said that court documents or docket activity were not used (three chief probation and pretrial services offices and one judge). The remaining 102 comments either mentioned a court document (the most common outcome) or were neutral with respect to court documents but focused on another source to identify a cooperator, typically the details of a specific incident. Those comments that did not explicitly mention court documents focused instead on other sources for identifying cooperators including "social media," "rats.com," "YouTube," or more generally "the internet." Of course, talk within a community, newspapers, movement in and out of the prison, and prior knowledge of the cooperator were also mentioned as sources of identification.

A final category of comments meriting further consideration was policy comments made by respondents. The twenty-nine respondents offering specific policy comments covered two dimensions. First are those who commented on whether a national policy was necessary or not. Seven of the twenty-nine respondents made comments about a national judiciary policy that could be considered negative in tone (four judges and three defenders). Included in this group were respondents' explicitly negative comments, such as "the need for blanket rules . . . is a canard," as well as more cautionary comments, such as "be sensitive to the public right to know." Other policy comments were more positive, suggesting a need for policy, though four suggested that this was an issue for the Department of Justice (DOJ) or, more specifically, the Bureau of Prisons (BOP) to address (three judges and one chief probation and pretrial services office). For instance, one respondent noted that the DOJ and the U.S. Attorney's Office do not consider protection of cooperators to be a priority, but they should. One comment noted that past efforts to work with BOP on this issue had not been successful. Seventeen other respondents suggested there was a need for national policy, made by the judiciary, or that the judiciary should do "something" about the issue. One judicial respondent's comment combined both elements, suggesting that this was a DOJ/BOP issue about which the judiciary needed to be concerned and take action.

Overall, while specific policy comments were rare, relative to the other types of comments provided, their tone could be categorized as suggesting a need for something to be done to protect cooperators. This is especially true if we consider all the comments as a group. In addition to the policy comments noted above, seventy-six respondents spoke about life in prison for cooperators, or prison culture in general, clearly noting a problem where there is an expectation of harm in prison for those who do cooperate or are unable to prove that they did not. These respondents consistently told a story of new inmates reporting to a specific individual (the "shot caller") in the prison and being required to provide their "paperwork" within a few weeks of coming to prison. If the inmates for any reason were unable to prove they were not a cooperator, they were told to request protective custody. These concerns prompted inmates to request their docket information, or (in the case of those who did cooperate) go so far as to request fake documents to protect them in prison.

Moreover, the general comments about the frequency of harm more often suggested that threat or harm was a frequent occurrence, and this was true even after including in our count those respondents who said they had nothing to report. Further, the steps reported for protecting defendants, witnesses, and (in one case) juries, suggest that the concerns about harm are real enough for districts to make affirmative steps to better protect cooperators from harm. Despite these efforts, respondents noted that there continue to be problems. The fear of being harmed or threatened is affecting the willingness of defendants and witnesses to cooperate, a comment made by 26 respondents (with one defender/panel representative's office as the exception). Taken as a whole, but certainly not unanimously, the open-ended comments support the results reported above: harm is occurring, court documents are often the sources for identifying cooperators, and this is a problem for the criminal justice system.

Conclusion

To answer the question of how often cooperators, both defendants/offenders and witnesses, were harmed, we surveyed federal district judges, U.S. Attorney's Offices, the offices of the federal defenders and CJA district panel representatives, and chief probation and pretrial services offices. With a 71% response rate, and representation from all 94 judicial districts, we are confident that the reported results are representative of the harm experienced by witnesses and defendants/offenders in the past three years. These groups reported a substantial amount of harm. Overall, respondents reported a minimum of 571 cases involving harm or threat. These instances of harm involved a minimum of 381 defendants/offenders and 292 witnesses; often, both were involved in the same case. Respondents reported a minimum of an additional 236 defendants/offenders and 301 witnesses harmed, but limits placed on the survey prevent us from knowing the details of such harm.

Respondents reported that the nature of harm or threat to defendants/offenders and witnesses was largely the same. Threats of physical harm and threats to friends or family occurred most frequently, and many respondents reported multiple types of threat made against the same defendant/offender or witness. It is worth noting, however, that defendants/offenders were more likely to be subject to multiple types of threat than witnesses were, though this difference could be the result of the availability of the information to our respondent groups.

We found, not surprisingly, that the location differed for defendants/offenders and witnesses when harmed or threatened. Defendants were most often in some form of custody (pretrial detention, pretrial release, or incarceration) while witnesses were not likely to be in custody, or, if they were in custody, they were in pretrial detention as a codefendant.

The sources for identifying cooperation by defendants/offenders and witnesses also differed somewhat, according to our respondents. While court documents and proceedings were overwhelmingly the source for identifying both types of cooperators, the specific sources are different. Defendants/offenders were identified in plea agreements, 5K1.1 motions, or through general docketing practices, especially the presence of a number of sealed CM/ECF docket entries or a sentencing reduction. Respondents also reported discovery and testimony as common sources for identifying defendant/offender cooperators. We found that witnesses, while also identified through court documents, were often identified through witness lists, because they give testimony in open court, or through discovery.

Respondents also reported on the willingness of defendants/offenders and witnesses to provide cooperating information. Defense attorneys as well as prosecutors reported that, in the past three years, hundreds of defendants/offenders and witnesses withdrew offers of cooperation and refused cooperation out of concerns about harm or threat. These results are echoed in the open-ended comments of these two groups as well. Concerns about harm are so real defendants requested court documents to prove they were not a cooperator over 1,900 times in the past three years.

While respondents were able to report on specific instances of harm or threat in the past three years, they were largely unable to compare the amount of harm in 2014 to 2013. When they did answer, they reported similar levels of harm across the two years.

The final question, asked of chief district judges, sought to identify policy changes that might be considered to protect cooperating defendants/offenders and witnesses. As reported by respondents, the district courts have adopted a number of measures in an attempt to protect cooperators. Among these measures is the sealing of docket entries such as plea agreements, often *sua sponte*, to shield cooperation information. Some districts have taken the additional step of docketing all criminal cases the same way—for example, docketing blank sealed documents where no cooperation occurred. Respondents' answers to questions about sources used to identify cooperators, especially defendants/offenders, raise questions about the effectiveness of such steps. Although sealing documents may seem like a logical solution to protecting information about cooperators, the presence of sealed documents and gaps in docket sequence numbers by themselves are considered enough by other inmates to identify cooperators and put them at risk of harm. The open-ended comments describe this phenomenon in detail. In these comments, respondents noted the problems inherent in sealing and made additional suggestions for protecting cooperating information, including a separate filing system for the public from that used by the courts. A small set of comments questioned the need for any policy for protecting cooperator information, as well as raising issues of public access to court documents and proceedings. We include all these suggestions in Appendix I.

Though the direction that policy should take is not clear from the information provided in this survey, the scope of the problem is. Respondents reported a substantial amount of harm, to both defendants and witnesses, resulting from use of court documents to identify cooperators. The problem occurs both during criminal prosecutions and once defendants (whether they cooperated or not) begin serving sentences in BOP and other facilities. Efforts to protect cooperating information, while in some instances successful, have not eliminated the problem of harm to cooperators. While respondents recognized that limiting access to these court documents would not completely eliminate harm to cooperators, there was general agreement that something needed to be done—by the judiciary, BOP, or both—to better protect cooperating information and reduce the risk of harm to defendants and witnesses assisting in criminal prosecutions.

Appendix A: Survey Invitation and Questionnaires

Dear ${m://Title} ${m://LastName}:

There is a growing concern that information contained in publicly accessible court documents is being used to threaten or harm defendants in criminal cases because of their cooperation or suspected cooperation with the government. Some courts have already acted in a variety of ways to safeguard such documents.

We write as the chairs of three Judicial Conference Committees to ask for your help in collecting information that will assist our committees in making an important policy decision – whether to propose to the Judicial Conference the establishment of national procedures for protecting information in court documents indicating a defendant's cooperation, or intent to cooperate, with the government.

In an effort to measure the extent of this problem, we have asked the Federal Judicial Center to conduct a survey on our behalf to gather information on threats of harm to, or actual harm suffered by, defendants and witnesses in criminal cases because they were actual or suspected cooperators with the government.

District judges, federal prosecutors and defenders, CJA district panel representatives, and chief probation and pre-trial officers are being surveyed.

When you click on the link below, you will connect to the survey. It will provide important information about how to respond. **Please be assured that all survey responses will be confidential and reported to the committees only in the aggregate.**

Thank you for your time. Your participation is greatly appreciated. Click on the link below to begin the survey. **Please complete the survey by March 17th, 2015.**

Sincerely,
Wm. Terrell Hodges, Chair
Court Administration and Case Management Committee

Irene M. Keeley, Chair
Criminal Law Committee

Catherine C. Blake, Chair
Defender Services Committee

Follow this link to the Survey:
${l://SurveyLink?d=Take the Survey}

Or copy and paste the URL below into your internet browser:
${l://SurveyURL}

Survey Instructions

Scope of the Survey. This survey asks about information you may have received regarding harm or threats of harm to defendants or witnesses on your docket because of their actual or perceived cooperation with the government. Please consider only defendants or witnesses from cases on your docket, not those of a colleague, and report information you consider to be reliable. Please consider only instances of harm or threats of harm from cases on your docket in the last three years.

Definition of "Harm." "Harm" refers to:

- Actual or threats of economic harm
- Actual or threats of physical harm
- Murder

suffered by a defendant or witness (or their friends or family), inflicted by a third party in retaliation for cooperating (or for being suspected of cooperating) with the government. Harm can occur at any point in a case, from pre-trial through conviction or acquittal or any time thereafter.

Confidentiality. All survey responses will be kept confidential and results will be reported only in the aggregate. Please do not identify any defendant or witness by name.

Who to Contact. If you have any questions about the study, you may contact any of the three committee chairs or Dr. Margaret Williams, who is directing the study. If you have questions about the items in this survey, or technical problems with the questionnaire, Dr. Williams can be reached at 202-502-4080 or mwilliams@fjc.gov.

In cases on your docket over the past three years, have you learned of any defendants and/or witnesses who were harmed or threatened (including harm or threats to friends or family) because of the defendant's or witness' cooperation with the government?

○ Yes

○ No

○ I can't recall

Please think about the cases from the last three years for which you have the most information about actual harm or threats of harm to defendants or witnesses (or their friends or family). **This questionnaire asks a series of questions on up to five cases from your docket.** While you may not have all the information on each case, please answer as many questions as you can to provide a complete picture of the harm or threats of harm to each person.

[NOTE THIS SECTION WILL REPEAT UP TO FIVE TIMES.]

Thinking about the first case, who was harmed or threatened with harm? (Check all that apply)

❑ Defendant

❑ Witness

Did the defendant experience any of the following types of harm or threats? (Choose one per row)

	Yes	No	Have no knowledge
Threats of economic harm	○	○	○
Actual economic harm	○	○	○
Threats of physical harm	○	○	○
Actual physical harm	○	○	○
Murder	○	○	○
Threats to friends or family	○	○	○
Actual harm to friends or family	○	○	○
Other (please specify)	○	○	○

When the defendant was harmed or threatened, he/she was... (Choose one per row)

	Yes	No	Have no knowledge
in pre-trial detention	O	O	O
on pre-trial release	O	O	O
incarcerated post-conviction	O	O	O
in an RRC or halfway house	O	O	O
on probation or supervised release	O	O	O
elsewhere (please specify)	O	O	O

Did the defendant request protective custody or placement in a special housing unit?
O Yes
O No
O I can't recall

Did the defendant receive protective custody or placement in a special housing unit?
O Yes
O No
O I can't recall

Were any of the following court documents used to identify the defendant as a cooperator (or suspected cooperator) with the government? (Choose one per row)

	Yes	No	Have no knowledge
Judicial opinion	O	O	O
Rule 35(b) motion	O	O	O
§ 5K1.1 motion testimony/transcript	O	O	O
Plea agreement or plea supplement	O	O	O
Sentencing memorandum	O	O	O
Other (please specify)	O	O	O

Did the witness experience any of the following types of harm or threats? (Choose one per row)

	Yes	No	Have no knowledge
Threats of economic harm	O	O	O
Actual economic harm	O	O	O
Threats of physical harm	O	O	O
Actual physical harm	O	O	O
Murder	O	O	O
Threats to friends or family	O	O	O
Actual harm to friends or family	O	O	O
Other (please specify)	O	O	O

When the witness was harmed or threatened, he/she was... (Choose one per row)

	Yes	No	Have no knowledge
in pre-trial detention	O	O	O
on pre-trial release	O	O	O
incarcerated post-conviction	O	O	O
in an RRC or halfway house	O	O	O
on probation or supervised release	O	O	O
elsewhere (please specify)	O	O	O

Were any of the following court documents used to identify the witness as a cooperator (or suspected cooperator) with the government? (Choose one per row)

	Yes	No	Have no knowledge
Judicial opinion	○	○	○
Rule 35(b) motion	○	○	○
§ 5K1.1 motion testimony/transcript	○	○	○
Plea agreement or plea supplement	○	○	○
Sentencing memorandum	○	○	○
Other (please specify)	○	○	○

Are there other cases on your docket from the past three years in which you learned of a defendant or witness being harmed or threatened?
○ Yes
○ No
○ I can't recall

[NOTE: THIS IS THE END OF THE REPEATING SECTION]

Not including the defendants regarding whom you've provided information in this survey, how many more defendants from cases on your docket have you learned were harmed or threatened in the past three years?

Not including the witnesses regarding whom you've provided information in this survey, how many more witnesses from cases on your docket have you learned were harmed or threatened in the past three years?

Was the number of defendants and/or witnesses harmed or threatened due to perceived or actual cooperation with the government higher or lower in 2014 compared to 2013?
○ Higher in 2014
○ About the same in 2014
○ Lower in 2014
○ I don't know

To the best of your knowledge, what steps, if any, has your district taken to better protect cooperation information in court documents? (Check all that apply)

- ❑ Making criminal cases appear identically on CM/ECF to obscure cooperation information (such as requiring filing sealed supplements with a plea agreement)
- ❑ Sealing documents containing cooperation information sua sponte
- ❑ Sealing documents containing cooperation information at the request of the parties
- ❑ Ordering parties to redact cooperation information from documents
- ❑ Restricting remote access of documents containing cooperation information
- ❑ Allowing public access of documents containing cooperation information only in the courthouse or clerk's office
- ❑ Removing documents containing cooperation information from public files
- ❑ Requiring the entry of documents containing cooperation to be private entries in CM/ECF
- ❑ Other (please specify) _____
- ❑ None of the above

Please use the space below to provide any additional information about harm or threats of harm experienced by defendants and/or witnesses (or their family or friends) from cases on your docket in the past three years.

Survey Instructions

Scope of the Survey. This survey asks about information you may have received regarding harm or threats of harm to defendants or witnesses on your docket because of their actual or perceived cooperation with the government. Please consider only defendants or witnesses from cases on your docket, not those of a colleague, and report information you consider to be reliable. Please consider only instances of harm or threats of harm from cases on your docket in the last three years.

Definition of "Harm." "Harm" refers to:

- Actual or threats of economic harm
- Actual or threats of physical harm
- Murder

suffered by a defendant or witness (or their friends or family), inflicted by a third party in retaliation for cooperating (or for being suspected of cooperating) with the government. Harm can occur at any point in a case, from pre-trial through conviction or acquittal or any time thereafter.

Confidentiality. All survey responses will be kept confidential and results will be reported only in the aggregate. Please do not identify any defendant or witness by name.

Who to Contact. If you have any questions about the study, you may contact any of the three committee chairs or Dr. Margaret Williams, who is directing the study. If you have questions about the items in this survey, or technical problems with the questionnaire, Dr. Williams can be reached at 202-502-4080 or mwilliams@fjc.gov.

In cases on your docket over the past three years, have you learned of any defendants and/or witnesses who were harmed or threatened (including harm or threats to friends or family) because of the defendant's or witness' cooperation with the government?
- Yes
- No
- I can't recall

Please think about the cases from the last three years for which you have the most information about actual harm or threats of harm to defendants or witnesses (or their friends or family). **This questionnaire asks a series of questions on up to five cases from your docket.** While you may not have all the information on each case, please answer as many questions as you can to provide a complete picture of the harm or threats of harm to each person.

[NOTE THIS SECTION WILL REPEAT UP TO FIVE TIMES.]

Thinking about the first case, who was harmed or threatened with harm? (Check all that apply)
- Defendant
- Witness

Did the defendant experience any of the following types of harm or threats? (Choose one per row)

	Yes	No	Have no knowledge
Threats of economic harm	O	O	O
Actual economic harm	O	O	O
Threats of physical harm	O	O	O
Actual physical harm	O	O	O
Murder	O	O	O
Threats to friends or family	O	O	O
Actual harm to friends or family	O	O	O
Other (please specify)	O	O	O

When the defendant was harmed or threatened, he/she was... (Choose one per row)

	Yes	No	Have no knowledge
in pre-trial detention	O	O	O
on pre-trial release	O	O	O
incarcerated post-conviction	O	O	O
in an RRC or halfway house	O	O	O
on probation or supervised release	O	O	O
elsewhere (please specify)	O	O	O

Did the defendant request protective custody or placement in a special housing unit?
- O Yes
- O No
- O I can't recall

Did the defendant receive protective custody or placement in a special housing unit?
- O Yes
- O No
- O I can't recall

Were any of the following court documents used to identify the defendant as a cooperator (or suspected cooperator) with the government? (Choose one per row)

	Yes	No	Have no knowledge
Judicial opinion	O	O	O
Rule 35(b) motion	O	O	O
§ 5K1.1 motion testimony/transcript	O	O	O
Plea agreement or plea supplement	O	O	O
Sentencing memorandum	O	O	O
Other (please specify)	O	O	O

Did the witness experience any of the following types of harm or threats? (Choose one per row)

	Yes	No	Have no knowledge
Threats of economic harm	O	O	O
Actual economic harm	O	O	O
Threats of physical harm	O	O	O
Actual physical harm	O	O	O
Murder	O	O	O
Threats to friends or family	O	O	O
Actual harm to friends or family	O	O	O
Other (please specify)	O	O	O

When the witness was harmed or threatened, he/she was... (Choose one per row)

	Yes	No	Have no knowledge
in pre-trial detention	O	O	O
on pre-trial release	O	O	O
incarcerated post-conviction	O	O	O
in an RRC or halfway house	O	O	O
on probation or supervised release	O	O	O
elsewhere (please specify)	O	O	O

Were any of the following court documents used to identify the witness as a cooperator (or suspected cooperator) with the government? (Choose one per row)

	Yes	No	Have no knowledge
Judicial opinion	O	O	O
Rule 35(b) motion	O	O	O
§ 5K1.1 motion testimony/transcript	O	O	O
Plea agreement or plea supplement	O	O	O
Sentencing memorandum	O	O	O
Other (please specify)	O	O	O

Are there other cases on your docket from the past three years in which you learned of a defendant or witness being harmed or threatened?
O Yes
O No
O I can't recall

[NOTE THIS IS THE END OF THE REPEATING SECTION]

Not including the defendants regarding whom you've provided information in this survey, how many more defendants from cases on your docket have you learned were harmed or threatened in the past three years?

Not including the witnesses regarding whom you've provided information in this survey, how many more witnesses from cases on your docket have you learned were harmed or threatened in the past three years?

Was the number of defendants and/or witnesses harmed or threatened due to perceived or actual cooperation with the government higher or lower in 2014 compared to 2013?
O Higher in 2014
O About the same in 2014
O Lower in 2014
O I don't know

Please use the space below to provide any additional information about harm or threats of harm experienced by defendants and/or witnesses (or their family or friends) from cases on your docket in the past three years.

Cooperators - Federal Defenders and CJA Panel Representatives Preview

Survey Instructions

Scope of the Survey. This survey asks about information you may have received regarding harm or threats of harm to defendants or witnesses because of their actual or perceived cooperation with the government. Please consider only defendants or witnesses from your cases, not those of a colleague, and report information you or your staff consider to be reliable. Please consider only instances of harm or threats of harm from cases in the last three years. We ask that you coordinate the responses among the members of your office to create a single response for the entire office. Please do not forward the survey link.

Definition of "Harm." "Harm" refers to:

- Actual or threats of economic harm
- Actual or threats of physical harm
- Murder

suffered by a defendant or witness (or their friends or family), inflicted by a third party in retaliation for cooperating (or for being suspected of cooperating) with the government. Harm can occur at any point in a case, from pre-trial through conviction or acquittal or any time thereafter.

Confidentiality. All survey responses will be kept confidential and results will be reported only in the aggregate. Please do not identify any defendant or witness by name.

Who to Contact. If you have any questions about the study or technical problems with the questionnaire, please contact Dr. Margaret Williams at 202-502-4080 or mwilliams@fjc.gov.

In your cases over the past three years, have you learned of any defendants and/or witnesses who were harmed or threatened (including harm or threats to friends or family) because of the defendant's or witness' cooperation with the government?

O Yes

O No

O I can't recall

Please think about the cases from the last three years for which you have the most information about actual harm or threats of harm to defendants or witnesses (or their friends or family). **This questionnaire asks a series of questions on up to five cases.** While you may not have all the information on each case, please answer as many questions as you can to provide a complete picture of the harm or threats of harm to each person.

[NOTE THIS SECTION WILL REPEAT UP TO FIVE TIMES.]

Thinking about the first case, who was harmed or threatened with harm? (Check all that apply)

❑ Defendant

❑ Witness

Did the defendant experience any of the following types of harm or threats? (Choose one per row)

	Yes	No	Have no knowledge
Threats of economic harm	O	O	O
Actual economic harm	O	O	O
Threats of physical harm	O	O	O
Actual physical harm	O	O	O
Murder	O	O	O
Threats to friends or family	O	O	O
Actual harm to friends or family	O	O	O
Other (please specify)	O	O	O

When the defendant was harmed or threatened, he/she was... (Choose one per row)

	Yes	No	Have no knowledge
in pre-trial detention	O	O	O
on pre-trial release	O	O	O
incarcerated post-conviction	O	O	O
in an RRC or halfway house	O	O	O
on probation or supervised release	O	O	O
elsewhere (please specify)	O	O	O

Did the defendant request protective custody or placement in a special housing unit?
O Yes
O No
O I can't recall

Did the defendant receive protective custody or placement in a special housing unit?
O Yes
O No
O I can't recall

Were any of the following court documents used to identify the defendant as a cooperator (or suspected cooperator) with the government? (Choose one per row)

	Yes	No	Have no knowledge
Judicial opinion	O	O	O
Rule 35(b) motion	O	O	O
§ 5K1.1 motion testimony/transcript	O	O	O
Plea agreement or plea supplement	O	O	O
Sentencing memorandum	O	O	O
Other (please specify)	O	O	O

Did the witness experience any of the following types of harm or threats? (Choose one per row)

	Yes	No	Have no knowledge
Threats of economic harm	O	O	O
Actual economic harm	O	O	O
Threats of physical harm	O	O	O
Actual physical harm	O	O	O
Murder	O	O	O
Threats to friends or family	O	O	O
Actual harm to friends or family	O	O	O
Other (please specify)	O	O	O

When the witness was harmed or threatened, he/she was... (Choose one per row)

	Yes	No	Have no knowledge
in pre-trial detention	O	O	O
on pre-trial release	O	O	O
incarcerated post-conviction	O	O	O
in an RRC or halfway house	O	O	O
on probation or supervised release	O	O	O
elsewhere (please specify)	O	O	O

Were any of the following court documents used to identify the witness as a cooperator (or suspected cooperator) with the government? (Choose one per row)

	Yes	No	Have no knowledge
Judicial opinion	O	O	O
Rule 35(b) motion	O	O	O
§ 5K1.1 motion testimony/transcript	O	O	O
Plea agreement or plea supplement	O	O	O
Sentencing memorandum	O	O	O
Other (please specify)	O	O	O

Are there other cases from the past three years in which you learned of a defendant or witness being harmed or threatened?
O Yes
O No
O I can't recall

[NOTE: THIS IS THE END OF THE REPEATING SECTION]

Not including the defendants regarding whom you've provided information in this survey, how many more defendants from your cases have you learned were harmed or threatened in the past three years?

Not including the witnesses regarding whom you've provided information in this survey, how many more witnesses from your cases have you learned were harmed or threatened in the past three years?

In the past three years, how many defendants, because of actual or threatened harm, requested case information (CM/ECF docket, pre-sentence report, etc.) to prove they were not a cooperator?

In the past three years, how many defendants, because of actual or threatened harm, requested all or part of their CM/ECF docket be sealed?

In the past three years, how many defendants withdrew offers of cooperation because of actual or threatened harm?

In the past three years, how many defendants refused cooperation because of actual or threatened harm?

In the past three years, how many witnesses withdrew offers of cooperation because of actual or threatened harm?

In the past three years, how many witnesses refused cooperation because of actual or threatened harm?

Was the number of defendants and/or witnesses harmed or threatened due to perceived or actual cooperation with the government higher or lower in 2014 compared to 2013?
- ○ Higher in 2014
- ○ About the same in 2014
- ○ Lower in 2014
- ○ I don't know

Please use the space below to provide any additional information about harm or threats of harm experienced by defendants and/or witnesses (or their family or friends) from your cases in the past three years.

Survey Instructions

Scope of the Survey. This survey asks about information you may have received regarding harm or threats of harm to defendants/offenders or witnesses from your district because of their actual or perceived cooperation with the government. Please consider only defendants/offenders or witnesses from your district and report information you or your staff consider to be reliable. Please consider only instances of harm or threats of harm from cases from your district in the last three years. We ask that you coordinate the responses among the members of your office to create a single response for the entire office. Please do not forward the survey link.

Definition of "Harm." "Harm" refers to:

- Actual or threats of economic harm
- Actual or threats of physical harm
- Murder

suffered by a defendant/offender or witness (or their friends or family), inflicted by a third party in retaliation for cooperating (or for being suspected of cooperating) with the government. Harm can occur at any point in a case, from pre-trial through conviction or acquittal or any time thereafter.

Confidentiality. All survey responses will be kept confidential and results will be reported only in the aggregate. Please do not identify any defendant/offender or witness by name.

Who to Contact. If you have any questions about the study or technical problems with the questionnaire, please contact Dr. Margaret Williams at 202-502-4080 or mwilliams@fjc.gov.

In cases from your district over the past three years, have you learned of any defendants/offenders and/or witnesses who were harmed or threatened (including harm or threats to friends or family) because of the defendant/offender's or witness' cooperation with the government?

○ Yes
○ No
○ I can't recall

Please think about the cases from the last three years for which you have the most information about actual harm or threats of harm to defendants/offenders or witnesses (or their friends or family). **This questionnaire asks a series of questions on up to five cases.** While you may not have all the information on each case, please answer as many questions as you can to provide a complete picture of the harm or threats of harm to each person.

[NOTE THIS SECTION WILL REPEAT UP TO FIVE TIMES.]

Thinking about the first case, who was harmed or threatened with harm? (Check all that apply)

❑ Defendant/Offender
❑ Witness

Did the defendant/offender experience any of the following types of harm or threats? (Choose one per row)

	Yes	No	Have no knowledge
Threats of economic harm	○	○	○
Actual economic harm	○	○	○
Threats of physical harm	○	○	○
Actual physical harm	○	○	○
Murder	○	○	○
Threats to friends or family	○	○	○
Actual harm to friends or family	○	○	○
Other (please specify)	○	○	○

When the defendant/offender was harmed or threatened, he/she was... (Choose one per row)

	Yes	No	Have no knowledge
in pre-trial detention	O	O	O
on pre-trial release	O	O	O
incarcerated post-conviction	O	O	O
in an RRC or halfway house	O	O	O
on probation or supervised release	O	O	O
elsewhere (please specify)	O	O	O

Did the defendant/offender request protective custody or placement in a special housing unit?
- O Yes
- O No
- O I can't recall

Did the defendant/offender receive protective custody or placement in a special housing unit?
- O Yes
- O No
- O I can't recall

Were any of the following court documents used to identify the defendant/offender as a cooperator (or suspected cooperator) with the government? (Choose one per row)

	Yes	No	Have no knowledge
Judicial opinion	O	O	O
Rule 35(b) motion	O	O	O
§ 5K1.1 motion testimony/transcript	O	O	O
Plea agreement or plea supplement	O	O	O
Sentencing memorandum	O	O	O
Other (please specify)	O	O	O

Did the witness experience any of the following types of harm or threats? (Choose one per row)

	Yes	No	Have no knowledge
Threats of economic harm	○	○	○
Actual economic harm	○	○	○
Threats of physical harm	○	○	○
Actual physical harm	○	○	○
Murder	○	○	○
Threats to friends or family	○	○	○
Actual harm to friends or family	○	○	○
Other (please specify)	○	○	○

When the witness was harmed or threatened, he/she was... (Choose one per row)

	Yes	No	Have no knowledge
in pre-trial detention	○	○	○
on pre-trial release	○	○	○
incarcerated post-conviction	○	○	○
in an RRC or halfway house	○	○	○
on probation or supervised release	○	○	○
elsewhere (please specify)	○	○	○

Were any of the following court documents used to identify the witness as a cooperator (or suspected cooperator) with the government? (Choose one per row)

	Yes	No	Have no knowledge
Judicial opinion	○	○	○
Rule 35(b) motion	○	○	○
§ 5K1.1 motion testimony/transcript	○	○	○
Plea agreement or plea supplement	○	○	○
Sentencing memorandum	○	○	○
Other (please specify)	○	○	○

Are there other cases from your district in the past three years in which you learned of a defendant or witness being harmed or threatened?
- ○ Yes
- ○ No
- ○ I can't recall

[NOTE: THIS IS THE END OF THE REPEATING SECTION]

Not including the defendants/offenders regarding whom you've provided information in this survey, how many more defendants/offenders from cases in your district have you learned were harmed or threatened in the past three years?

Not including the witnesses regarding whom you've provided information in this survey, how many more witnesses from cases in your district have you learned were harmed or threatened in the past three years?

Was the number of defendants/offenders and/or witnesses harmed or threatened due to perceived or actual cooperation with the government higher or lower in 2014 compared to 2013?
- ○ Higher in 2014
- ○ About the same in 2014
- ○ Lower in 2014
- ○ I don't know

Please use the space below to provide any additional information about harm or threats of harm experienced by defendants/offenders and/or witnesses (or their family or friends) from cases in your district in the past three years.

Survey Instructions

Scope of the Survey. This survey asks about information you may have received regarding harm or threats of harm to defendants or witnesses because of their actual or perceived cooperation with the government. Please consider only defendants or witnesses from cases prosecuted by your office, not those of a colleague, and report information you consider to be reliable. Please consider only instances of harm or threats of harm from cases in the last three years. We ask that you coordinate the responses among the members of your office to create a single response for the entire office. Please do not forward the survey link.

Definition of "Harm." "Harm" refers to:

- Actual or threats of economic harm
- Actual or threats of physical harm
- Murder

suffered by a defendant or witness (or their friends or family), inflicted by a third party in retaliation for cooperating (or for being suspected of cooperating) with the government. Harm can occur at any point in a case, from pre-trial through conviction or acquittal or any time thereafter.

Confidentiality. All survey responses will be kept confidential and results will be reported only in the aggregate. Please do not identify any defendant or witness by name.

Who to Contact. If you have questions about the items in this survey, or technical problems with the questionnaire, please contact Dr. Margaret Williams at 202-502-4080 or mwilliams@fjc.gov.

In cases prosecuted by your office over the past three years, have you learned of any defendants and/or witnesses who were harmed or threatened (including harm or threats to friends or family) because of the defendant's or witness' cooperation with the government?

○ Yes
○ No
○ I can't recall

Please think about the cases from the last three years for which you have the most information about actual harm or threats of harm to defendants or witnesses (or their friends or family). **This questionnaire asks a series of questions on up to five cases.** While you may not have all the information on each case, please answer as many questions as you can to provide a complete picture of the harm or threats of harm to each person.

[NOTE THIS SECTION WILL REPEAT UP TO FIVE TIMES.]

Thinking about the first case, who was harmed or threatened with harm? (Check all that apply)
❑ Defendant
❑ Witness

Did the defendant experience any of the following types of harm or threats? (Choose one per row)

	Yes	No	Have no knowledge
Threats of economic harm	○	○	○
Actual economic harm	○	○	○
Threats of physical harm	○	○	○
Actual physical harm	○	○	○
Murder	○	○	○
Threats to friends or family	○	○	○
Actual harm to friends or family	○	○	○
Other (please specify)	○	○	○

When the defendant was harmed or threatened, he/she was... (Choose one per row)

	Yes	No	Have no knowledge
in pre-trial detention	O	O	O
on pre-trial release	O	O	O
incarcerated post-conviction	O	O	O
in an RRC or halfway house	O	O	O
on probation or su-pervised release	O	O	O
elsewhere (please specify)	O	O	O

Did the defendant request protective custody or placement in a special housing unit?
O Yes
O No
O I can't recall

Did the defendant receive protective custody or placement in a special housing unit?
O Yes
O No
O I can't recall

Were any of the following court documents used to identify the defendant as a cooperator (or suspected cooperator) with the government? (Choose one per row)

	Yes	No	Have no knowledge
Judicial opinion	O	O	O
Rule 35(b) motion	O	O	O
§ 5K1.1 motion testi-mony/transcript	O	O	O
Plea agreement or plea supplement	O	O	O
Sentencing memoran-dum	O	O	O
Other (please specify)	O	O	O

Did the witness experience any of the following types of harm or threats? (Choose one per row)

	Yes	No	Have no knowledge
Threats of economic harm	○	○	○
Actual economic harm	○	○	○
Threats of physical harm	○	○	○
Actual physical harm	○	○	○
Murder	○	○	○
Threats to friends or family	○	○	○
Actual harm to friends or family	○	○	○
Other (please specify)	○	○	○

When the witness was harmed or threatened, he/she was... (Choose one per row)

	Yes	No	Have no knowledge
in pre-trial detention	○	○	○
on pre-trial release	○	○	○
incarcerated post-conviction	○	○	○
in an RRC or halfway house	○	○	○
on probation or supervised release	○	○	○
elsewhere (please specify)	○	○	○

Were any of the following court documents used to identify the witness as a cooperator (or suspected cooperator) with the government? (Choose one per row)

	Yes	No	Have no knowledge
Judicial opinion	O	O	O
Rule 35(b) motion	O	O	O
§ 5K1.1 motion testimony/transcript	O	O	O
Plea agreement or plea supplement	O	O	O
Sentencing memorandum	O	O	O
Other (please specify)	O	O	O

Are there other cases prosecuted by your office in the past three years in which you learned of a defendant or witness being harmed or threatened?

O Yes

O No

O I can't recall

[NOTE: THIS IS THE END OF THE REPEATING SECTION]

Not including the defendants regarding whom you've provided information in this survey, how many more defendants from cases prosecuted by your office have you learned were harmed or threatened in the past three years?

Not including the witnesses regarding whom you've provided information in this survey, how many more witnesses from cases prosecuted by your office have you learned were harmed or threatened in the past three years?

In the past three years, how many defendants withdrew offers of cooperation because of actual or threatened harm?

In the past three years, how many defendants refused cooperation because of actual or threatened harm?

In the past three years, how many witnesses withdrew offers of cooperation because of actual or threatened harm?

In the past three years, how many witnesses refused cooperation because of actual or threatened harm?

Was the number of defendants and/or witnesses harmed or threatened due to perceived or actual cooperation with the government higher or lower in 2014 compared to 2013?

- ○ Higher in 2014
- ○ About the same in 2014
- ○ Lower in 2014
- ○ I don't know

Please use the space below to provide any additional information about harm or threats of harm experienced by defendants and/or witnesses (or their family or friends) from cases prosecuted by your office in the past three years.

Appendix B: Other Types of Harm or Threat to Defendants

Categories of Other Harm	Description
Property damage	Animal
Property damage	destruction of property
Property damage	homes or automobiles [shot] at while occupied
Property damage	property damage
Property damage	The home that he and his family resided in was shot up a day before he was scheduled to testify
Property damage	Family house shot at
Property damage	Shot window out of residence
Property damage	they burned his house down
Property damage	Defendant's home was fired upon by unknown individual.
Internet/community/general threats	One offender [redacted] claims to have been shot at leaving the Residential Reentry Center after providing a drug test. A second [offender] [redacted] advised she had repeated threats at the gas station where [she worked] and on Facebook postings. A third offender [redacted] [is receiving] threats in the community and on [Facebook].
Internet/community/general threats	isolation at prison due to threats
Internet/community/general threats	made uncomfortable
Internet/community/general threats	Potential threat due to offender at RRC testifying against another offender's brother
Internet/community/general threats	Believed he [cooperated] but did not and he continues to receive threats
Internet/community/general threats	Although not physically harmed, defendant was physically grabbed when the threat was made against him.
Internet/community/general threats	Defendant's status as a cooperator was put on the internet.
Internet/community/general threats	Flyers posted in his neighborhood that he cooperated.
Internet/community/general threats	Name posted on Top Snitches Facebook page
Internet/community/general threats	told family members to put his name on rats.com
Internet/community/general threats	After testifying against co-defendants, intimidated via activity around home
Internet/community/general threats	Note on floor [of] halfway house identifying defendant as cooperator
Internet/community/general threats	person contacted offender's mother at her residence and his wife, via Facebook, and make some veiled verbal threats and name calling

Categories of Other Harm	Description
Internet/community/general threats	Intimidation; showed up at work and in the neighborhood
Internet/community/general threats	veiled threats via text message
Internet/community/general threats	Video / YouTube Rap Video Threat
Existing categories	One offender [redacted] claims to have been shot at leaving the Residential Reentry Center after providing a drug test. A second [offender] [redacted] advised she had repeated threats at the gas station where [she worked] and on Facebook postings. A third offender [redacted] is receiving threats in the community and on [Facebook].
Existing categories	Implications of cultural beliefs/acts that may harm defendant/offender and family
Existing categories	Arson of mother's house killed six people
Existing categories	Shot 3 times
Existing categories	[Threats] were made regarding the safety and welfare of defendant's family members in [redacted]
Existing categories	As with the last question answered, I have had multiple defendants in pretrial detention face threats for themselves or family members abroad if they proceeded to cooperate
Existing categories	Cultural beliefs/acts that may harm defendant and family.
Existing categories	In [immigration] drug cases routinely defendant and family are threats by drug lords
Existing categories	was assaulted in the middle of trial testimony
Other	Especially true in codefendants' providing substantial assistance
Other	threats to prosecution and defense counsel
Other	[Missing Comment]
Other	Media and Courtroom Testimony
Other	relocated 4 times

Appendix C: Other Locations at the Time of Harm or Threat to Defendants

Categories of Other Locations	Description
Not in custody of any kind	after completion of imprisonment and supervised release
Not in custody of any kind	less than a year following his termination of supervised release
Not in custody of any kind	Not arrested
Not in custody of any kind	not charged
Not in custody of any kind	post conviction and [sentence]
Not in custody of any kind	the defendant was harmed prior to being charged due to his cooperation
Not in custody of any kind	Witness- out of custody
Not in custody of any kind	not yet charged
Not in custody of any kind	upon release
Not in custody of any kind	one cooperator was uncharged at the time of the threat
Not in custody of any kind	pre-arrest
Not in custody of any kind	Prior to arrest - narc traffickers in [redacted]
Not in custody of any kind	non-incarcerated family members in [redacted]
Other forms of custody	pre sentencing release
Other forms of custody	state custody on another charge
Other forms of custody	witness protection program
Other forms of custody	Threats were numerous, starting while on bond and continuing into time on probation.
Other forms of custody	While awaiting sentencing.
Other forms of custody	The defendant was arrested on new criminal charges.
Other forms of custody	USMS lock-up pending a court proceeding
Other forms of custody	Custody
Other forms of custody	in [redacted] following deportation while on supervised release
Other forms of custody	USMS lock-up pending court proceeding
Other	During the course of the investigation
Other	For family members none of these applies
Other	I don't remember

Categories of Other Locations	Description
Other	defendant absconded pretrial release supervision and was living in [redacted]
Other	the threat - made to defendant - was of harm to his himself or his family
Other	[missing comment]
Other	suspected cooperating witness during drug conspiracy

Appendix D: Other Sources to Identify Defendants

Categories of Other Sources	Description
Suspicion	After the target's arrest, the defendant was suspected of cooperating. When the defendant was arrested (and in pre-trial detention) he was threatened. I took proactive steps to prevent disclosure of information during the court proceedings.
Suspicion	co-defendant suspicion
Suspicion	co-defendant [suspicions]
Suspicion	Defendant in an [redacted] RICO gang case was suspected by other incarcerated gang members of cooperating with law enforcement as to the murder of a police officer, and he was stabbed in a federal detention facility.
Suspicion	gossip
Suspicion	gossip
Suspicion	prison gossip
Suspicion	rumor
Suspicion	rumor of cooperation
Suspicion	rumor of cooperation
Suspicion	The Defendant was released with conditions and the co [defendants] were under the belief that anyone released was cooperating with the [government].
Suspicion	word of mouth
Other court document/proceeding	302 report after debriefing
Other court document/proceeding	a criminal complaint unsealed in a related case identified statements made by the defendant upon his arrest
Other court document/proceeding	A plea agreement that was not filed and was presumed to include a substantial assistance provision because it was filed under seal
Other court document/proceeding	a request letter to the judge to use the offender as an informant
Other court document/proceeding	A tape recorded conversation between the D and the CI was disclosed in discovery. Other Defendants obtained a copy of that recorded call and threatened the D and her family as a result.
Other court document/proceeding	affidavit

Categories of Other Sources	Description
Other court document/proceeding	After live testimony
Other court document/proceeding	Again, it is an issue with BOP inmates obtaining Docket Sheets.
Other court document/proceeding	BOP inmates demanded the defendant's docket sheet, and looked for "holes" in the docket sheet-- which corresponded to sealed motions, plea agreement attachments, sentencing memorandum, and the like. From those sealed docket entries, they correctly surmised the defendant was a cooperator.
Other court document/proceeding	Change in Offender's length of time listed in BOP data base
Other court document/proceeding	CI Agreement
Other court document/proceeding	co-defendant discovery
Other court document/proceeding	Community became aware client would testify at trial of co-defendants. Threats were then made to defendant and family
Other court document/proceeding	court-ordered discovery
Other court document/proceeding	Courtroom testimony
Other court document/proceeding	courtroom testimony
Other court document/proceeding	Courtroom [testimony]
Other court document/proceeding	Criminal Complaint
Other court document/proceeding	criminal complaint
Other court document/proceeding	DEA 6
Other court document/proceeding	debrief statement provided in discovery to target's [attorney]
Other court document/proceeding	Defendant did NOT cooperate but was threatened until produced clean docket sheet as proof
Other court document/proceeding	Defendant's cooperation was noted in a memorandum of interview that was produced to the defense in discovery. Report is that members of criminal organization will attend sentencing to hear if there are any references to cooperation.
Other court document/proceeding	Defendant's Motion to Vacate
Other court document/proceeding	disclosure of cooperation in discovery to codefendant
Other court document/proceeding	disclosure pre-trial
Other court document/proceeding	Discovery
Other court document/proceeding	Discovery

Categories of Other Sources	Description
Other court document/proceeding	Discovery
Other court document/proceeding	Discovery
Other court document/proceeding	discovery
Other court document/proceeding	Discovery
Other court document/proceeding	Discovery
Other court document/proceeding	Discovery
Other court document/proceeding	Discovery
Other court document/proceeding	discovery
Other court document/proceeding	Discovery
Other court document/proceeding	Discovery
Other court document/proceeding	Discovery Documents
Other court document/proceeding	discovery documents
Other court document/proceeding	discovery file
Other court document/proceeding	discovery file
Other court document/proceeding	discovery file
Other court document/proceeding	discovery file
Other court document/proceeding	discovery from co-defendant
Other court document/proceeding	discovery in state case
Other court document/proceeding	discovery information
Other court document/proceeding	Discovery material
Other court document/proceeding	Discovery material was distributed into community.
Other court document/proceeding	discovery materials
Other court document/proceeding	Discovery materials
Other court document/proceeding	Discovery materials
Other court document/proceeding	Discovery materials to codefendants
Other court document/proceeding	Discovery of co-defendants
Other court document/proceeding	discovery provided to counsel of codefendants
Other court document/proceeding	Discovery provided to the party who issued the threat
Other court document/proceeding	discussion during sentencing
Other court document/proceeding	docket
Other court document/proceeding	Docket entries would allow inference

Categories of Other Sources	Description
Other court document/proceeding	docket entry scheduling change of plea
Other court document/proceeding	docket reports of filings under seal
Other court document/proceeding	docket sheet
Other court document/proceeding	docket sheet
Other court document/proceeding	Docket sheet
Other court document/proceeding	docket sheet
Other court document/proceeding	Docket sheet had sealed filings
Other court document/proceeding	ECF-docket report
Other court document/proceeding	everything sealed
Other court document/proceeding	evidence and transcripts from co-defendant's trial
Other court document/proceeding	evidence at co-defendant's trial
Other court document/proceeding	FBI 302
Other court document/proceeding	Gave testimony on conduct of others within prison setting.
Other court document/proceeding	government witness list
Other court document/proceeding	Grand jury transcript.
Other court document/proceeding	He testified in a public trial but he was transported with the people against whom he testified.
Other court document/proceeding	I read about the issue in the PSR
Other court document/proceeding	in PSR & SOR
Other court document/proceeding	[indictment]
Other court document/proceeding	indictment
Other court document/proceeding	indictment
Other court document/proceeding	inference from docket entry
Other court document/proceeding	J&C, Presentence Report
Other court document/proceeding	J&C, Presentence Report
Other court document/proceeding	J&S, docket sheet - sealed documents
Other court document/proceeding	J&S, presence of sealed items on docket
Other court document/proceeding	Jencks
Other court document/proceeding	Judgment obviously reflecting a reduction from a mandatory minimum
Other court document/proceeding	Letter from counsel
Other court document/proceeding	memos with redactions

Categories of Other Sources	Description
Other court document/proceeding	Modification of Pretrial Conditions of Release Order
Other court document/proceeding	motion for transfer
Other court document/proceeding	motion practice
Other court document/proceeding	Motion to Seal - sealed justification
Other court document/proceeding	Motion to Seal-sealed justification
Other court document/proceeding	NJ state discovery
Other court document/proceeding	[observers] at plea and sentencing
Other court document/proceeding	Of these documents, only the [redacted] Circuit opinion publicly identified defendant as a cooperator; however BOP inmates confronted the defendant and obtained a copy of his Docket sheet, which showed gaps in entries for sealed documents. From these gaps, BOP inmates correctly deduced defendant had cooperated.
Other court document/proceeding	Order Setting Conditions of Release
Other court document/proceeding	Police report provided in discovery
Other court document/proceeding	police report, co-defendant
Other court document/proceeding	Presentence Investigation
Other court document/proceeding	Presentence Investigation
Other court document/proceeding	Presentence Investigation Report
Other court document/proceeding	presentence report
Other court document/proceeding	presentence report
Other court document/proceeding	presentence report
Other court document/proceeding	Proffer
Other court document/proceeding	Proffer agreement, GJ testimony in discovery file
Other court document/proceeding	proffer statements
Other court document/proceeding	Proffer-DEA Released to defense attorneys.
Other court document/proceeding	Prosecutor's Statement and quotes copied from PSI
Other court document/proceeding	Prosecutor's Statement or copies of PSI
Other court document/proceeding	PSR
Other court document/proceeding	PSR
Other court document/proceeding	PSR
Other court document/proceeding	PSR
Other court document/proceeding	PSR, GJ, Discovery

Categories of Other Sources	Description
Other court document/proceeding	PSR, GJ, Discovery
Other court document/proceeding	PSR, GJ, Discovery
Other court document/proceeding	related state court documents
Other court document/proceeding	report of proffer
Other court document/proceeding	Rule 16 discovery (search warrant affidavit—although the defendant was referred to generally as CS. I took proactive steps to seal other information to prevent additional disclosure.
Other court document/proceeding	scheduling a change of plea appearing on the docket
Other court document/proceeding	search warrant affidavit
Other court document/proceeding	sentencing transcript
Other court document/proceeding	sentencing transcript
Other court document/proceeding	Statement of Reason
Other court document/proceeding	Statement of Reasons
Other court document/proceeding	Statement of Reasons
Other court document/proceeding	Statement of Reasons
Other court document/proceeding	Statement of Reasons
Other court document/proceeding	statement to police
Other court document/proceeding	Suspected source was an ATF report provided in discovery as Jencks material prior to a suppression hearing.
Other court document/proceeding	Testified against co-defendants
Other court document/proceeding	testified in public trial
Other court document/proceeding	testified vs co- deft.
Other court document/proceeding	Testimony and Media
Other court document/proceeding	Testimony at trial
Other court document/proceeding	The defendant was believed to be a cooperator because he was on bond (after a drug arrest) when the main target of the investigation was arrested.

Categories of Other Sources	Description
Other court document/proceeding	[T]he defendant was forced to sign a letter requesting docket sheets. These docket sheets were to be used to determine whether the defendant cooperated with the [government]. The letters of request were sent to the US Probation Office and the Clerk's Office. [We] [redacted] chose not to send the requested documents to the defendant. The defendant's mother contacted the probation officer [who] wrote the pre-sentence report to advise of threats being made against her son (the defendant).
Other court document/proceeding	The defendant's name was noted in the grand jury testimony on a state case in which she provided testimony as a witness and received credit for on her federal case.
Other court document/proceeding	[T]he document being requested was the docket sheet which specifically indicates if the documents are sealed. We chose not to send the defendant his docket sheet as he requested.
Other court document/proceeding	The Presentence Report
Other court document/proceeding	[Trial] court paperwork would be used to determine if defendant had a 5K1.1
Other court document/proceeding	transcript/discovery
Other court document/proceeding	transcript/discovery
Other court document/proceeding	transcripts/discovery
Other court document/proceeding	transfer of inmate to attend court
Other court document/proceeding	trial testimony
Other court document/proceeding	trial testimony
Other court document/proceeding	trial testimony
Other court document/proceeding	Trial witness list
Other court document/proceeding	trial witness list
Other court document/proceeding	Under seal hearing in magistrate court
Other court document/proceeding	under seal not disclosed
Other court document/proceeding	witness disclosure
Other court document/proceeding	witness list
Other court document/proceeding	witness list
Other court document/proceeding	Witness lists
Other court document/proceeding	Witness lists
Other court document/proceeding	writ

Categories of Other Sources	Description
Other court document/proceeding	writ
Other court document/proceeding	writ
Other court document/proceeding	writted back
News	A newspaper article regarding the plea was published in [redacted]. The article made reference to my client's cooperation and named one of the person against whom he cooperated.
News	[newspaper] report about trial
News	Newspaper
News	Newspaper article
News	Government Detention Motion - which was quoted in news article
Talking to agents/debriefs/ government disclosure	At initial arrest, deft was seen talking to agents by his co-defendants.
Talking to agents/debriefs/ government disclosure	Defendant at government's request called drug distributor while he was under detention
Talking to agents/debriefs/ government disclosure	Defendant was identified because he came to the courthouse for debriefs on days when he did not have a scheduled court hearing.
Talking to agents/debriefs/ government disclosure	FBI advised PO/offender
Talking to agents/debriefs/ government disclosure	Government disclosure
Talking to agents/debriefs/ government disclosure	Government's disclosure of the defendant's cooperation in other unrelated cases.
Talking to agents/debriefs/ government disclosure	Govt. revealed cooperation in preparation of trial
Talking to agents/debriefs/ government disclosure	Jailhouse observation
Talking to agents/debriefs/ government disclosure	Observed cooperating
Talking to agents/debriefs/ government disclosure	questioning by FBI
Talking to agents/debriefs/ government disclosure	The defendant provided [information] that was used by law enforcement to contact the person. The law enforcement contact was used as identification that the defendant was a cooperator.
Talking to agents/debriefs/ government disclosure	Trips out of jail to proffer, where no court hearing was scheduled.

Categories of Other Sources	Description
Talking to agents/debriefs/ government disclosure	Was pulled from the facility for multiple debriefs with agents.
Talking to agents/debriefs/ government disclosure	Was pulled from the jail and brought to meet with agents.
Co-defendants/known	codefendant
Co-defendants/known	Co-defendant
Co-defendants/known	direct threat [from] father against his son in person
Co-defendants/known	Ex-boyfriend
Co-defendants/known	from a co-defendant
Co-defendants/known	info from other co-defendants
Co-defendants/known	info from others involved in case
Co-defendants/known	info from witnesses in case
Co-defendants/known	Information [received] from other defendants
Co-defendants/known	known cooperation
Co-defendants/known	One defendant's attorney told the attorney for another defendant of his [client's] cooperation
Co-defendants/known	statements by co-conspirators
Co-defendants/known	The defendant is one of many defendants in a large [redacted] gang prosecution. Cooperators in this gang are routinely murdered. This defendant has pleaded guilty and everything possible is being done to assure his safety, including the use of sealed filings and proceedings
Co-defendants/known	The defendant self-identified himself as cooperating against a co-defendant
Other	A 5K1.1 [motion] was filed but the defendant was shot prior to the sentencing. It is no exactly clear as to how the defendant was identified as a cooperator.
Other	extra-judicial knowledge
Other	Murdered due to cooperation
Other	narcotics traffickers in [redacted]
Other	Not sure. Was killed within a day or two of arrival at prison.
Other	other

Categories of Other Sources	Description
Other	The defendant was believed to be cooperating (post-indictment); daughter (who was believed to be an anonymous source to law enforcement) was assaulted. I took proactive steps to prevent the disclosure of sensitive documents.
Other	Unknown
Other	[Unknown]
Other	USAO submitted
Other	Was FBI Informant

Appendix E: Other Types of Harm or Threat to Witnesses

Categories of Other Harm	Description
Attempted murder	Attempt to Murder
Attempted murder	contract to kill witness
Attempted murder	Defendant [solicited] the killing of witness
Other	[missing comment]
Other	Agents developed information that the defendant was associated with a gang and was part of a plan to kill an ATF agent and an AUSA.
Other	defendant was going to be a witness
Other	Disclosure of suspicion that person was a cooperator
Other	economic harm to family
Other	free world
Other	Other
Other	Other
Other	promise of gifts for favorable testimony
Other	relocation
Other	same as mentioned earlier
Other	Same person
Other	The person was not a defendant in the particular criminal action but was perceived by defendants as a cooperator. The perceived witness was in custody on a different matter.
Other	The witness was the defendant who cooperated and testified
Other	under seal
Internet/community/general threats	3rd party [harassment]
Internet/community/general threats	being ostracized by defendant's family and community
Internet/community/general threats	[harassment] of sex trafficking victim by posting pictures
Internet/community/general threats	identity of cooperator posted on [YouTube]
Internet/community/general threats	nonspecific threats via social media

Categories of Other Harm	Description
Internet/community/general threats	threat that defendant would sue the witness for defamation or other civil money damages or that the witness could be prosecuted for perjury if willing to testify against the defendant
Internet/community/general threats	threatened by defendant
Internet/community/general threats	threatened multiple times
Property damage	destruction of property
Property damage	homes and automobiles [shot] up while occupied
Property damage	The witness' apartment was burned
Property damage	Witness' home was riddled with bullets from a high-powered weapon and a child was narrowly missed on the eve of the witness/ testimony.
Existing categories	In this case, the [threatening] conduct occurred prior to the arrest and was part of the criminal conduct/charges. There was a threat of physical harm to a potential witness.
Existing categories	threats of murder

Appendix F: Other Locations at the Time of Harm or Threat to Witnesses

Categories of Other Locations	Description
Not in custody	A victim not under Court supervision and not in custody
Not in custody	abroad
Not in custody	At his workplace
Not in custody	at home
Not in custody	at home
Not in custody	at home - not accused
Not in custody	at large
Not in custody	at [liberty] with no pending charges
Not in custody	at liberty
Not in custody	at place of employment
Not in custody	at residence
Not in custody	Case not yet charged
Not in custody	[civilian] witness
Not in custody	[civilian] witness
Not in custody	[civilian] witness
Not in custody	Community
Not in custody	community
Not in custody	Community
Not in custody	Community
Not in custody	cooperating witness
Not in custody	FBI agent
Not in custody	Free
Not in custody	free
Not in custody	Free
Not in custody	Free
Not in custody	Free from custody
Not in custody	free world
Not in custody	free world

Categories of Other Locations	Description
Not in custody	Had not yet been charged. She was cooperating with the government.
Not in custody	Home
Not in custody	home
Not in custody	Home
Not in custody	Home
Not in custody	home - not a co-conspirator
Not in custody	Home and Work
Not in custody	home and work
Not in custody	Home and Work
Not in custody	Home and work
Not in custody	Home and Work-FBI Case Agent
Not in custody	Home County
Not in custody	in community
Not in custody	in community/not [an] offender
Not in custody	in his/her community
Not in custody	in his/her community
Not in custody	in home
Not in custody	In home or automobile
Not in custody	In one case a [defendant's] former lawyer was threatened with [murder]. In another a bank robbery witness was killed two weeks post trial. Was a brother of the defendant who was acquitted.
Not in custody	in the community
Not in custody	in the community
Not in custody	informant was not in custody; he was a paid CI
Not in custody	living at home
Not in custody	living at home
Not in custody	living at home
Not in custody	living at home
Not in custody	living in the community where the other defendants lived
Not in custody	Living with a suspect
Not in custody	living with Defendant [(fiancée)]

Categories of Other Locations	Description
Not in custody	lured away from her home by defendant
Not in custody	no pending charges
Not in custody	No pending charges
Not in custody	non-defendant
Not in custody	non-incarcerated family member of witness and witness
Not in custody	non-incarcerated family members
Not in custody	normal residence
Not in custody	Not arrested
Not in custody	not arrested
Not in custody	Not charged
Not in custody	not charged
Not in custody	Not charged
Not in custody	Not charged
Not in custody	not charged. cooperating with government
Not in custody	not facing charges
Not in custody	NOT IN ANY KIND OF CUSTODY
Not in custody	not in custody
Not in custody	Not in custody
Not in custody	not in custody
Not in custody	Not in custody
Not in custody	Not in custody
Not in custody	Not in custody
Not in custody	not in custody- not charged
Not in custody	not in custody though had an attorney and was attempting to cooperate
Not in custody	Not in custody.
Not in custody	not in [custody]
Not in custody	Not under Court supervision or custody
Not in custody	On street
Not in custody	on the street
Not in custody	On the street.
Not in custody	on the streets

Categories of Other Locations	Description
Not in custody	on the streets
Not in custody	on the streets
Not in custody	out
Not in custody	out of custody
Not in custody	out of custody
Not in custody	out of custody witness
Not in custody	public
Not in custody	some witnesses were not charged.
Not in custody	Someone fired a gun at a confidential informant in a bar after his picture was posted online identifying him as the source for a defendant's indictment
Not in custody	the assailant and witness were not locked up
Not in custody	The threat of harm occurred prior to the initial arrest.
Not in custody	The [threatening] conduct occurred prior to the initial arrest of the defendant.
Not in custody	The witness was not charged with a crime
Not in custody	The witness was not charged with any crime
Not in custody	the witness wasn't in the criminal [system]
Not in custody	trial witness, not in custody
Not in custody	Uncharged
Not in custody	under investigation
Not in custody	under investigation
Not in custody	[unindicted] witness not in custody
Not in custody	[non-incarcerated] witness
Not in custody	[non-incarcerated] witness
Not in custody	was a trial witness
Not in custody	was a witness
Not in custody	was just witness
Not in custody	Was not charged
Not in custody	while in the community
Not in custody	Witness in Community
Not in custody	Witness not charged
Not in custody	Witness not charged

Categories of Other Locations	Description
Not in custody	Witness not charged
Not in custody	Witness not in custody
Not in custody	witness not in system
Not in custody	witness was a citizen
Not in custody	Witness was a [redacted] Police officer in the murder of a [law enforcement officer]. He testified at pre-trial hearings in a hood and with the courtroom closed. The case involved in the death of the agent and the elimination of 3 to 5 other [redacted] that were aware of the circumstances leading up to the [officer's] killing.
Not in custody	witness was an informant and a police officer giving information about police corruption
Not in custody	witness was an informant living in society
Not in custody	witness was an informant who was shot at
Not in custody	witness was at liberty
Not in custody	witness was child victim
Not in custody	witness was the victim
Not in custody	witnesses not in system
Other	[missing comment]
Other	a business owner
Other	co-defendants, criminal
Other	confidential source
Other	cooperator
Other	court-ordered discovery
Other	defense attorneys were threatened
Other	For family members none of these applies
Other	I had a person convicted of sexual assault threaten the victim's family after a jury verdict
Other	in courtroom testifying
Other	in [redacted]
Other	in state court proceeding
Other	Individual was a member of organized crime.
Other	known to defendant
Other	paid cooperator

Categories of Other Locations	Description
Other	returned to the danger zone
Other	still in the conspiracy
Other	The person was a cooperating witness for the government who may have been a coconspirator as well as friend of defendant but do not know if government ever charged cooperator.
Other	under seal
Other	was a confidential informant
Other	witness protection
Existing category	It is my understanding that the witness was on supervised release
Existing category	Post conviction release
Existing category	Post-plea pre-sentence release
Existing category	the witness, a gang member, testified for the government in a trial before one of my colleagues. The witness would have been a witness in my court in a case related to similar issues, but he was murdered [redacted]. The witness was not in custody at the time of his death, but I believe he was on supervised release.

Appendix G: Other Sources to Identify Witnesses

Categories of Other Sources	Description
Suspicion	all were by word of mouth that he was a cooperator
Suspicion	jail house talk
Suspicion	rumor
Suspicion	suspicion of [co-conspirators]
Suspicion	The witness was murdered [because] it was believed that he was a snitch
Suspicion	word of mouth
Suspicion	word on street
Other court document/proceeding	affidavit
Other court document/proceeding	All documents reflecting cooperation are sealed.
Other court document/proceeding	announced as a witness during the trial
Other court document/proceeding	ATF Agent's Report
Other court document/proceeding	Audio tapes that were used to charge an obstruction count.
Other court document/proceeding	believe child protective services call disclosed cooperation
Other court document/proceeding	case is pending; witness roles revealed in discovery
Other court document/proceeding	Change of plea notice on ECF
Other court document/proceeding	co-defendant discovery
Other court document/proceeding	complaint
Other court document/proceeding	Court testimony
Other court document/proceeding	Court testimony
Other court document/proceeding	court-ordered discovery
Other court document/proceeding	court-ordered discovery
Other court document/proceeding	Criminal Complaint
Other court document/proceeding	Criminal Complaint
Other court document/proceeding	criminal complaint
Other court document/proceeding	Deduced from docket sheet
Other court document/proceeding	Defendant learned that witness appeared before grand jury
Other court document/proceeding	discovery
Other court document/proceeding	discovery

Categories of Other Sources	Description
Other court document/proceeding	discovery
Other court document/proceeding	discovery
Other court document/proceeding	discovery
Other court document/proceeding	discovery
Other court document/proceeding	Discovery
Other court document/proceeding	discovery
Other court document/proceeding	Discovery
Other court document/proceeding	discovery
Other court document/proceeding	Discovery
Other court document/proceeding	Discovery
Other court document/proceeding	discovery
Other court document/proceeding	Discovery
Other court document/proceeding	discovery
Other court document/proceeding	Discovery
Other court document/proceeding	Discovery
Other court document/proceeding	discovery
Other court document/proceeding	Discovery
Other court document/proceeding	Discovery
Other court document/proceeding	discovery
Other court document/proceeding	Discovery
Other court document/proceeding	discovery
Other court document/proceeding	Discovery Documents
Other court document/proceeding	Discovery documents — Agent reports
Other court document/proceeding	discovery material
Other court document/proceeding	Discovery material
Other court document/proceeding	discovery materials
Other court document/proceeding	discovery materials
Other court document/proceeding	Discovery provided to defense counsel for the person against whom the witness testified.
Other court document/proceeding	Discovery revealed identity
Other court document/proceeding	discovery to defendant
Other court document/proceeding	Docket Sheets
Other court document/proceeding	fact of sealed filings

Categories of Other Sources	Description
Other court document/proceeding	fact of sealed filings
Other court document/proceeding	FBI 302
Other court document/proceeding	FBI 302
Other court document/proceeding	FBI 302 and trial testimony
Other court document/proceeding	Grand Jury testimony & discovery
Other court document/proceeding	grand jury transcript
Other court document/proceeding	grand jury transcripts/discovery
Other court document/proceeding	Grand Jury Transcript
Other court document/proceeding	Gvmt witness list
Other court document/proceeding	identified in pretrial
Other court document/proceeding	identity of informant made clear by discovery
Other court document/proceeding	indictment
Other court document/proceeding	Informant was identified after video surveillance was produced by the [government] in discovery
Other court document/proceeding	informant's role made clear in discovery
Other court document/proceeding	Interview report provided in discovery
Other court document/proceeding	Investigation reports
Other court document/proceeding	Jencks Act Material turned over in advance of trial despite protective orders prohibiting defendant from keeping a copy in the jail
Other court document/proceeding	[Jencks] r. 16 materials
Other court document/proceeding	Letter from USAO to Defense Counsel
Other court document/proceeding	police report
Other court document/proceeding	police report
Other court document/proceeding	police report describing witnesses cooperation provided in discovery
Other court document/proceeding	Police reports
Other court document/proceeding	police reports
Other court document/proceeding	Police Reports and proffer statements
Other court document/proceeding	Possible the [redacted] Police report when one of the suspects was apprehended in [redacted].
Other court document/proceeding	Presentence report
Other court document/proceeding	presentence report
Other court document/proceeding	pretrial service report

Categories of Other Sources	Description
Other court document/proceeding	pretrial witness list
Other court document/proceeding	Proffer report provided in discovery
Other court document/proceeding	Prosecutor's Statement and copies of PSI
Other court document/proceeding	PSR
Other court document/proceeding	PSR
Other court document/proceeding	PSR
Other court document/proceeding	PSR
Other court document/proceeding	PSR
Other court document/proceeding	PSR
Other court document/proceeding	Public testimony as [cooperating witness]
Other court document/proceeding	recordings
Other court document/proceeding	related state court documents
Other court document/proceeding	role of witness made clear in discovery
Other court document/proceeding	role of witness made clear in discovery
Other court document/proceeding	rule to show cause hearing
Other court document/proceeding	saw investigation information
Other court document/proceeding	sealed trial witness list
Other court document/proceeding	search warrant
Other court document/proceeding	search warrant affidavit
Other court document/proceeding	sentencing docs
Other court document/proceeding	state complaint
Other court document/proceeding	state complaint and state search warrant
Other court document/proceeding	State court discovery and plea documents.
Other court document/proceeding	subpoena
Other court document/proceeding	testified against codefendant
Other court document/proceeding	Testified at trial
Other court document/proceeding	Testified in a Court Proceeding
Other court document/proceeding	Testifying
Other court document/proceeding	testimony
Other court document/proceeding	Testimony at hearings
Other court document/proceeding	Testimony at probable cause hearing
Other court document/proceeding	testimony in trial of co defendant

Categories of Other Sources	Description
Other court document/proceeding	testimony of the witness
Other court document/proceeding	The witness was threatened and then badly beaten following his testimony before me
Other court document/proceeding	The witness was verbally threatened in the [court-house], and was targeted as a [snitch] by use of Facebook and Instagram
Other court document/proceeding	the writ that identified him as a government witness was circulated at the jail
Other court document/proceeding	They were identified by not being publicly filed like codefendants' documents
Other court document/proceeding	transcript of trial
Other court document/proceeding	trial
Other court document/proceeding	trial testimony
Other court document/proceeding	Trial testimony
Other court document/proceeding	trial testimony
Other court document/proceeding	trial testimony
Other court document/proceeding	trial testimony
Other court document/proceeding	trial transcript
Other court document/proceeding	trial witness list
Other court document/proceeding	withdrawal from the case
Other court document/proceeding	withdrawal from the pending case
Other court document/proceeding	witness list provided in advance of trial pursuant to court order
Other court document/proceeding	Witness lists
Other court document/proceeding	Witness lists
Other court document/proceeding	Witness Statements
Other court document/proceeding	witness testified at trial
News	newspaper
Co-defendants/known	circumstances of drug sale
Co-defendants/known	cooperating co def
Co-defendants/known	defendant knew witness had disclosed information
Co-defendants/known	Defendant knew witness was present at time of crime and observed events
Co-defendants/known	in a [redacted] Mafia case the word got out that the wife of a co-conspirator was going to be a witness and she was [targeted] to be killed.

Categories of Other Sources	Description
Co-defendants/known	known to defendant
Co-defendants/known	known to defendant
Co-defendants/known	known to target
Co-defendants/known	known to target
Co-defendants/known	Named co-defendant in indictment
Co-defendants/known	source disclosure
Co-defendants/known	statement by defendant
Co-defendants/known	The witness was previously employed by the defendant, and he knew she planned to testify against him.
Co-defendants/known	unindicted co-conspirators
Co-defendants/known	usually identified as family members of the cooperating defendant
Talking to agents/debriefs/ government disclosure	Observation in jail
Talking to agents/debriefs/ government disclosure	Seen talking with authorities on a routine matter
Other	[missing comment]
Other	His lawyer disclosed
Other	I meant to share the following information as it relates to type of harm experienced by the witness. The victim was a witness in a criminal case in which her son was murdered. The victim (the young man's mother) was raped and nearly killed.
Other	Not sure how Marshal Service learned of the hit but the suspect was apprehended across the street from the court house at the time the [witness] was testifying,
Other	Not sure. he was killed within a day or two of arrival at prison
Other	on the streets
Other	Other
Other	other
Other	Other
Other	same as mentioned earlier
Other	under seal
Other	Was detained as a material witness in alien smuggling case.

Appendix H: Other Steps to Protect Cooperation Information

Other Steps Taken, Specified by Chief District Judges
Info regarding cooperation at plea or sentencing heard at sidebar and then sealed
Not mailing out PSRs on request.
sealed portions of transcripts in every guilty plea and sentencing
The cooperation provisions of a plea agreement are in a separate document, not filed with the Clerk of Court, and maintained only [by] the judge and the prosecutor and the defense attorney. Also, the prosecutor's sentencing memo describing cooperation is not filed—indeed even a non-cooperator's sentencing memo is not filed, so that there is no way to determine by deduction that a defendant "must" be a cooperator. Finally, any sentencing transcript is redacted for cooperating information before it is published on the docket.
unaware of clerk's procedures
US Attorney has taken steps to remove references to cooperation in hearings and documents. Court is discussing better ways to protect PSRs.
We have levels of access and access restriction and use those on a case by case basis.

Appendix I: Open-Ended Comments

Categories	Open-Ended Comments
Missing	[missing comment]
Nothing to report	[During] my tenure as a judge in the [redacted district], none of the defendants/witnesses in any of the criminal cases I presided over were ever harmed or threatened to my knowledge.
Nothing to report	I have handled only one criminal case in the past 8 years—and there were no threats in that one. Sorry I can't be of any help.
Takes issue with the survey	I am extremely uncomfortable participating in this survey. Your questions cross or come perilously close to crossing the line into attorney-client confidentiality. Had I possessed concrete information concerning harm or threats, I probably would have decided to assert the privilege. A lawyer is not likely to have acquired the type of information the survey seeks except by privileged communication, especially given the parameters the survey places on how to answer the question. It does not solve the problem to promise that the information will remain confidential; the disclosure is [to] be complete once the question is answered. In addition, your survey form demanded specific numerical answers. I do not keep records concerning this issue. So, in particular, my answer to the question "how many requests for file materials to show that they were not a cooperator?" is an estimate based upon my best recollection of the number of inquiries I might have received over the last several years. In a three year parameter, the number may very well be "1". Finally, in my experience, it is virtually impossible to quantify refusals to cooperate based upon threats to personal safety. There are a myriad of moral, ethical, legal and other factors, different in each case, that a client might weigh—and properly so—in reaching a decision about whether to provide information concerning associates. Because the question of whether to cooperate is intensely and uniquely personal, many lawyers, myself included, consider their fiduciary duty to be met by listing those factors and letting the client reflect upon them alone, or with loved ones. Decisions, as far as I can tell, are made after balancing all such factors. It is very rare that the decision is based upon any single one.

Categories	Open-Ended Comments
General comment about harm in prison/prison culture	The prison environment is very difficult and tense, both in my [redacted] and [redacted]. Paperwork is demanded, and people - even people who exerted a fair amount of power on the street - are genuinely intimidated.
Procedures for protecting defendants; general comments about the sources to identify cooperator	On [redacted], [redacted] adopted Standing Order Regarding Sealing Documents Filed in Criminal Matters. The Order provides prior authorization for the Clerk of Court to file, under seal, documents from pro se defendants seeking reduction of sentence based on cooperation. Filings by counsel under 5K1.1, Rule 35 and section 3553(e) must be accompanied by a motion to seal. [redacted]
Procedures for protecting defendants	The threatened person wrote the court advising of a threat. The court [conferred] with the defense atty and the Government atty. Also the court called the warden of the prison in the presence of the attorneys and made them aware of the alleged threat
Procedures for protecting defendants; general comment about the frequency of harm	I generally will ask defendants whether they or any member of their family has been threatened as a part of the plea colloquy in an [appropriate] case. Not infrequently they will either answer yes or no. If I think from the facts or [circumstances] that it is likely that threats have occurred I will ask whether they would tell me truthfully whether such a threat had been made. It happens [a lot] in drug and immigration related cases.
Details of a specific incident	I am aware of a large drug conspiracy case that involved a threat to a prosecutor and myself. The prosecutors in the case informed me that threats had been made against co-defendants in the case.
Details of a specific incident	I had a large number of defendants in a heroin case which involved two murders and several threats.
General comment about the frequency of harm	I have had 2 or 3 defendants explain why, as former felons, they possess weapons all the while knowing that doing so is a violation of their [supervised release]. On these occasions, the defendants have persuasively explained to me that gang members or other criminal actors threaten to kill the defendants if they will not re-engage with gang/criminal activities. They knowingly possess guns in violation of [supervised release] to protect themselves and family. This is not linked to perceived or actual cooperation with the government, but is responsive to the "additional information about harm or threats of harm...in the past three years."

Categories	Open-Ended Comments
Procedures for protecting witnesses	It is difficult to determine how many of our witnesses were harmed or threatened as a result of their cooperation in our cases. We take preventive measures to assure witness safety and often relocate witnesses as soon as they begin cooperating. There are times when our witnesses are threatened in their communities because they are suspected of cooperating or they are recognized by the defendant and threatened or harmed. When that happens we immediately bring them in and offer them relocation services. It is a rare case when our witnesses are identified as cooperators through court proceedings (other than at trial) or court documents because all such documents are placed under seal. Because the [redacted district] has a high witness retaliation rate, we wait until the last possible moment to disclose the names of our witnesses and cooperators.
General comment about the frequency of harm	It seems the perception of harm/ threat is greater earlier in the process, due to the associates co-defendants have made.
General comment about the frequency of harm; details of a specific incident; general comment about harm in prison/prison culture; general comments about the sources to identify cooperator	Most threats (real or perceived) are in drug cases. Defense attorneys routinely ask that absolutely no record of their clients' cooperation be shown anywhere in the record, including plea agreements and 5K1 motions. One defendant was so worried about being identified as a snitch that he asked to be sentenced to his statutory mandatory minimum [redacted] imprisonment) even though he qualified for a 5K1 motion at sentencing. He had been told by other defendants that when he showed up at his designated BOP facility, he would be asked to provide his Pre-Sentence Report or J&C as "proof" as to whether or not he was a rat.
Details of a specific incident; general comment about harm in prison/prison culture; general comment about the frequency of harm; general comments about the sources to identify cooperator	1) Social media has been used to post discovery. 2) We had one defendant who managed to get a criminal associate hired at the law firm of a co-defendant out of desperation to determine whether anyone was cooperating, including the co-defendant. 3) Inmates regularly abuse "legal mail" privileges to send written threats to witnesses and judges while in BOP custody; 4) We had a defendant go pro se in an attempt to undermine a protective order which limited dissemination of discovery; 5) We had to relocate a witness and their entire family after he was [threatened] at gunpoint; 6) We had a witness who was shot [at] by two males, each [carrying] a gun. Had they not missed, he would have been dead; 7) threats against judicial officers have required recusal of the USAO, necessitating appointment of an SAUSA and costly travel and lodging expenses. In one such case, our AUSA was required to make [redacted] overnight air trips to another District and was out of town in a hotel during [redacted] [a] long trial.

Categories	Open-Ended Comments
General comment about harm in prison/prison culture; general comment about the frequency of harm	A BOP investigator in a civil rights case testified in my court that upon entry into the FCIs he has worked in, new inmates are routinely and quickly confronted and made to produce their sentencing "paperwork" by a deadline to prove that they did not cooperate with authorities. The inmates are told that if they cannot do so, they should seek protective custody (usually by requesting transfer into the "secure" (maximum security) unit, or face violence from other inmates. An inmate corroborated this account.
Details of a specific incident; general comments about the sources to identify cooperator; procedures for protecting defendants	A co-defendant in a multi-defendant drug conspiracy flipped and testified for the Government. He was being housed in the Metropolitan Correctional Center on a different floor from the other defendants. One day during trial, the defendant and the cooperator were brought over in the same van.
Details of a specific incident; procedures for protecting defendants	A defendant in a drug conspiracy indictment before another judge in this district conspired with others to kidnap 2 defendants on pretrial release with cases before me, have the defendants transported to [redacted], then murdered. The 2 defendants cooperated with law enforcement, one posing for pictures as having been shot in a bathtub, and the government filed 5K motions for reduction.
Details of a specific incident	A defendant's home was burned down when his cooperation was made known. A mother and her daughter (both witnesses) were threatened with a gun and were directed to submit affidavits prepared by the defendant regarding why they would not testify before the grand jury. A defendant made it known that anyone who testified against him would be shunned in a small rural [community]. In a case in which a member of the conspiracy was murdered for stealing drugs, cooperators described pressure from Defendant and his family members to not submit to pressure from government.
Procedures for protecting defendants	Again, all the cases were filed under seal
Procedures for protecting defendants	All of my knowledge is anecdotal, and non-specific. We work hard to use preventive measures identified above to avoid these situations.
General comment about the frequency of harm	Almost all inmates request Docket. I am certain they are pressured to get that information but I know of no actual threats of harm that leads them to make this request.
General comment about the frequency of harm; general comment about harm in prison/prison culture	Almost all of our clients who are sentenced to incarceration call the office from the designated institution and request some court document to prove that they have not cooperated.
Nothing to report	Although the issue is occasionally raised in criminal cases I believe that the threat to family/friends was only remotely credible on one [occasion] and the specifics were lacking.

Categories	Open-Ended Comments
Details of a specific incident; procedures for protecting defendants; general comment about harm in prison/prison culture; general comments about the sources to identify cooperator	An offender under supervision reported being assaulted on more than one occasion while in BOP custody. Another offender under supervision reported being severely beaten while in BOP custody and threatened several times while on supervised release. One officer reported preparing presentence reports for a [redacted] defendant drug conspiracy where numerous defendants cooperated. The cooperation activities were only disclosed through confidential memorandums and sentencing memorandums filed under seal. The case agent and a defense attorney reported one cooperating defendant and his/her family received numerous violent threats from other codefendants and members of the community, which caused the cooperating defendant's family to move to another city. The defendant's name and the words "rat" or "snitch" was written numerous times on the walls of the Marshals' holding cells.
Nothing to report	As noted we have no documented instances of harm or threats in these types of cases so they were neither higher nor lower from one year to the next.
Takes issue with the survey	Asking how many defendants and witnesses refused cooperation is asking for an unknown, because we don't know if a defendant or witness was interested in cooperating or why they chose not to do so. We also do not know whether threats were directed to potential witnesses.
Details of a specific incident	[redacted] I presided over a trial of a heroin kingpin. All of his co-defendants pleaded guilty and none testified against him. However, one of the co-defendants had [a] death threat from a [redacted] cartel. This may have been because the co-defendant was suspected of cooperating with the government, although the co-defendant did not have a cooperation agreement provision in his written Plea Agreement.
Policy comments	Be [sensitive] to the public's right to know about the details of criminal cases even those that involve a potential for harm to cooperators.
General comment about the frequency of harm; details of a specific incident; general comments about the sources to identify cooperator	Before taking senior status, I had a fairly heavy criminal caseload. Given the number of cases, it is difficult for me to remember all the ones in which cooperating defendants and witnesses received threats. In 2014, for example, I held [redacted] sentencing hearings. Very few of those involved simple immigration cases. Most were drug conspiracies, fraud type offenses, and firearms offenses. There are often concerns in the drug cases about retaliation against cooperators. The drug gangs do their best to obtain court documents indicating who cooperates and who does not. I am sure that I have had many criminal defendants, their family members, and witnesses in criminal cases who have received threats. One was the victim of a drive-by shooting in retaliation.

Categories	Open-Ended Comments
General comment about the frequency of harm	Belligerent attitude among and between defendants and their respective witnesses has intensified; threatened murders of relatives of defendants is much more common and whether they have occurred may not be available information to the Court. Whatever "restraints" on behavior that may have previously existed, they have vanished!
Details of a specific incident; procedures for protecting defendants	Both of the offenders experienced threats of physical harm to self and family while on supervised release; and didn't request or receive protective custody of special housing unit placement.
General comment about the frequency of harm; general comment about harm in prison/prison culture; general comments about the sources to identify cooperator	Clients call to request PSR and court documents to document that they are not cooperating. I have recently heard that convicts are more apt to be requested info from other [redacted] inmates. I question whether convicts from [redacted] cooperate after conviction and threaten or force other [redacted] inmates to provide information proving that they are not "rats".
Details of a specific incident; general comment about harm in prison/prison culture	co-defendant died under suspicious circumstances while at the detention center
General comment about the frequency of harm; general comment about harm in prison/prison culture	Co-Defendants and witnesses who cooperate are often threatened even though their cooperation is to be confidential. [Occasionally] actual physical violence occurs. There is clearly an element of [intimidation] present in the detention and prison facilities.
General comment about harm in prison/prison culture; general comment about the frequency of harm; procedures for protecting defendants; procedures for protecting witnesses; details of a specific incident; general comments about the sources to identify cooperator	Comments offered by AUSAs: / / / Comment 1: Defense attorneys often ask about whether it is possible to leave cooperation out of plea agreements or to seal plea agreements. Defendants who are considering cooperation are concerned about the presence of sealed 5K motions being a red flag for cooperator status with other BOP inmates, and many fear general reprisal upon reaching the BOP. The above case is a good example of this prisoner notion of being considered "soft" if one is housed in prison with a "snitch." The defendant was suspected of having a gang connection to the ultimate instigator of the violence, but his accomplices were motivated to help simply in order to remove a cooperator from their midst, or to "check the snitch off the block." / / Comment 2: The threat of harm is always a major issue in prosecuting gang cases. It is difficult to determine when there have been actual threats that we do not know of, and when the reluctant witness fears retribution in the future, but nothing has been threatened yet. In general, a substantial number of potential witnesses to gang violence appear nervous about cooperating, and it takes a great deal of effort to get people to cooperate. / / Comment 3: We are seeing an increase in defense attorneys telling us that their clients don't want to cooperate nor do they want us to put a cooperation provision in their plea agreements – and are [leery] of sealed entries in their dock-

Categories	Open-Ended Comments
	et sheets because when they get to prison, the cooperation or sealed entries are taken to mean they are snitches. Not sure if they are concerned only about harm to themselves, but the harm to their families, especially those back home in [redacted]. / / Comment 4: I have one defendant who cooperated in a state case. He was never explicitly threatened, but life on the street doesn't require explicit threats. When we first met this defendant he refused to discuss the source of the counterfeit currency he was caught distributing. In fact, he got it from some gang members in [redacted] area, but wouldn't discuss it with us. He did tell us that he wouldn't talk about the currency because he knew that members of the gang would come after his mother. He was never threatened, but there was no need of a threat. / / I don't know exactly what the survey is trying to capture, but it's missing a big problem. There need not be an actual threat to shut down cooperation, as the above example shows. I recall other anecdotes but they're older than three years. / / Comment 5: Threats from the Cartels in [redacted] continue to be an issue. One defendant and her children were forced to flee and face prosecution here because of threats to her regarding possible cooperation of her and her husband. A material witness in that same case has been pursuing asylum from the Immigration Court out of [redacted]. /
General comment about the frequency of harm; general comment about harm in prison/prison culture; general comments about the sources to identify cooperator	cooperating defendants who are incarcerated are routinely asked to show their plea agreements to prove they are not cooperating with the government
Details of a specific incident	[redacted], who agreed to cooperate with the government, was murdered the very night of her first interview. Two defendants in a multi-defendant drug conspiracy case were charged with her murder. One was convicted by jury of murder, one pleaded guilty to the murder charge.
General comment about harm in prison/prison culture; general comment about the frequency of harm; policy comments; general comments about the sources to identify cooperator	Defendants are frequently confronted and asked to provide their Docket Sheet upon arrival at their BOP facility. That Docket Sheet is then examined by other inmates for sealed documents that create "gaps" in the Docket Sheet sequential numbering. Any gaps are viewed with suspicion--as the inmates usually correctly assume those are sealed motions, plea agreements, orders, and memorandum related to cooperation. The defendant is then labeled a cooperator. This forces the defendant into protective custody, or leads to assaults, harassment, threats, and other behavior. I have tried to work with BOP Legal Counsel to ban BOP inmates from having Docket Sheets (much like the BOP bans PSRs, which were excluded from inmate possession for similar reasons). I have not heard back from BOP legal counsel on the issue.

Categories	Open-Ended Comments
General comment about harm in prison/prison culture; general comment about the frequency of harm; details of a specific incident; general comments about the sources to identify cooperator	Defendants are threatened with bodily harm when they arrive at their designated institutions by the prisoners that are designated the "shot callers". Before the defendants are permitted to be on the yard, he must show his paper work, (plea agreement and judgment). Some have requested their presentence report which is not permitted in the possession of an inmate. One defendant was beaten so bad, he was hospitalized. He did not cooperate, but rather another inmate with the same name. The prisoners received the information after having had family and friends look up the defendant's name.
General comment about harm in prison/prison culture; general comments about the sources to identify cooperator	Demands by inmates for new inmates to supply a copy of their Plea Agreements and sentencing transcripts for verification that they were not cooperators. Failure to provide the required information meant they were considered to be "rats"
Details of a specific incident; procedures for protecting witnesses; procedures for protecting defendants	During our office's prosecution of multiple defendants who were part of a local [redacted] gang, a cooperating witness ("CW") was threatened with death, and so were members of his family in [redacted]. The Government arranged for members of the CW's family to be brought to the United States for their safety. Following their arrival, the Government provided funds for the CW's family members to change residences due to additional threats from the defendants. During this prosecution, eight of the defendants who cooperated with the Government sought and received custodial wit-sec protection due to likely retaliation and threat assessment. / / During our office's investigation of several gang members of [redacted] descent, 3 cooperating defendants were threatened while in custody. / / During our office's prosecution of several corrupt police officers involved in illegal drug activities, the confidential informant ("CI") was threatened via text message by one of the defendants. Prior to receipt of the threat, the Government had already arranged for the CI to be relocated out of state for his protection. /
Details of a specific incident; procedures for protecting witnesses; procedures for protecting defendants	Each of the cases that I have had involving witnesses have been victims of domestic violence where the defendant is on supervised release and I am informed that the defendant has threatened the victim. It is brought to my attention through a supervised release revocation report. The case with the cooperating defendant being threatened and put into protective custody was also brought to my attention due to a pretrial services officer informing me.
Policy comments; general comment about the frequency of harm; general comments about the sources to identify cooperator	Electronic dissemination of case information, particularly when informants are involved, is problematical for incarcerated defendants. It makes motion and appellate practice cumbersome, and it is nearly impossible to control sensitive information to the detriment of defendants and government witnesses as well. As a defense attorney, I much prefer that these matters not be publicized.

Categories	Open-Ended Comments
General comment about the frequency of harm; policy comments; general comments about the sources to identify cooperator	Every client sent to BOP asks for a copy of their docket sheet, even the clients who did cooperate. The cooperating clients want us to somehow amend the docket sheet so there are no sealed documents. Meanwhile, as someone who also represents the people who are cooperated against, I know that finding out information about cooperation efforts, even though it's important impeachment evidence, is becoming more and more difficult.
Nothing to report	Fear of the prosecutor and agents more prevalent fear.
Nothing to report	Fortunately, I have none to report
General comment about the frequency of harm	Have been a number of cases where illegal alien defendants were participants in drug distribution in U.S., usually as low-level couriers or mules, for a relatively nominal payment of money, but not otherwise a significant part of the drug operation. Many report having been threatened, or having their families threatened, in [redacted] by drug cartels operating there. The government has conceded, in at least some of the cases, that the threats and risks are real.
Details of a specific incident	Higher in 2014 due to Robbery Case where four Defendant's/witnesses were assaulted or threatened.
Nothing to report	I am a new Judge appointed in [redacted]
Nothing to report	I am a recently appointed judge, and have no criminal docket at this time.
Nothing to report; takes issue with the survey	I am not aware of any harm or threats in the past 3 years. Thus, in answering this question I was not sure whether to select "I don't know" or "about the same"....
Nothing to report	I am not aware of any instances where cooperators were threatened or harmed.
Nothing to report	I am not aware of any reported incidents or threats to defendants from our district.
Nothing to report; general comment about the frequency of harm	I am relatively new to the bench. But this has been going on for years.
Nothing to report	I am Senior Status and have not handled any criminal [cases] for the last three years.
General comment about the frequency of harm; general comment about harm in prison/prison culture; procedures for protecting witnesses; general comments about the sources to identify cooperator	I am very concerned about cooperating witnesses once they get to prison, whether they cooperated initially and received a benefit for cooperation at their initial sentencing or later got a Rule 35. Even though we try to protect them by sealing certain documents, allies of those who want to know for improper reasons can access the court file from outside of prison, and they do. When a sealed Order in an otherwise dormant file shows up, you can just about bet it is a Rule 35 reduction, and allies of others in prison know that. I had one instance of where I somehow found out about such an inquiry being made for others in prison.
Nothing to report	I began my service as a federal district court judge on [redacted]

Categories	Open-Ended Comments
Nothing to report	I believe I had one and possibly two alleged threats to family members, but all of it was hearsay and not much collaboration.
Takes issue with the survey; general comment about the frequency of harm; policy comments; general comments about the sources to identify cooperator	I believe the survey calls for speculative answers. To the extent such threats or harm can be linked [with] any court activity, which is speculative itself, if there is a link, it is the following: if anyone who wants to do harm to a so-called cooperator is sophisticated in any [respect], they know that the word "sealed" on any court docket means only one thing: a cooperation provision is part of the case. / The fact of cooperation cannot be kept from the public [vis-à-vis] the specifics of the cooperation. At sentencing the judge of course must announce the amount of time being reduced from the sentence for cooperation. The details of the cooperation are never placed on the record except in the rare case where the defendant chooses to.
General comment about the frequency of harm; general comments about the sources to identify cooperator	I believe there was a concern that threats are generated from those who gain access to public documents that discuss cooperation or potential cooperation by a defendant in custody.
General comment about the frequency of harm; comments about refusal out of fear	I can not recall threat of harm to cooperators but do recall 1) defendants and family members who [were] threatened/harassed because people thought the defendant was cooperating or might do so, and 2) defendants who declined to proffer and help [themselves] because people might think they were cooperators
Takes issue with the survey; general comment about the frequency of harm; general comment about harm in prison/prison culture; comments about refusal out of fear	I can only answer for defendants because that's whom we represent. I can't answer for witnesses. / Limit of 100 is insufficient to express number of defendants who 1) request court documents to show they didn't cooperate (virtually all of those incarcerated make this request, so many hundreds; 2) I can't quantify number of defendants who refuse to cooperate out of fear. This is a constant theme and vastly exceeds 100.

Categories	Open-Ended Comments
Nothing to report; general comment about the frequency of harm; policy comments	I cannot recall the last time a client, defendant or witness in a matter I was involved in was threatened in any way. In my practice, which overwhelmingly involves the representation of federal defendants and witnesses in federal criminal matters, the threat or risk of harm has not presented itself in years. The extent to which such is an issue depends on the nature of the case and the defendants involved in it. For example, in my district, the risk of harm to a cooperating defendant or witness in a health care fraud case is typically much lower than that faced by a similar defendant or witness in large scale drug trafficking case where the leaders of the conspiracy remain free while a low ranking conspirator is enlisted as witness in an ongoing investigation that has yet [to] result in additional arrests and charges against the leaders. I also perceive that defendants and witnesses in many cases, including drug trafficking and other organized criminal activities, are more likely to cooperate today than in the past. It is more common and there is less taboo therefore associated with "cooperating" among defendants and witnesses. The current mechanism whereby the parties must articulate to the court why something should be sealed appears to be working. The purported need for blanket rules allowing court records and documents to be sealed or shielded from the public is a canard.
Nothing to report	I can't recall any others
Takes issue with the survey; general comment about the frequency of harm; procedures for protecting defendants; general comments about the sources to identify cooperator; comments about refusal out of fear	I could not accurately answer the previous questions with a number. We frequently have clients call asking for their file and/or docket to prove they are not cooperators - even client who have cooperated. Most [do] not claim they are being threatened but some do. I cannot quantify how many call but it is often. Most ask that the cooperation portion of a plea agreement be placed under seal (that is not automatically done here). 5K motions and anything referencing cooperation (e.g. mtns to adjourn) are under seal. I cannot quantify. I will say that most often when they want to withdraw it is because they do not want to be exposed as a cooperator through testimony but not necessarily because they've already been threatened. It is a concern they will be threatened/harmed once their name is on a witness list. Since most cases plea, cooperators are not exposed. We also have clients who choose not to cooperate. Some make that choice because they do not want to help the government or turn on their family/friends. Others are scared of retaliation. I cannot quantify this because we do not necessarily ask our clients why they are making this decision. / / I don't know if this is helpful. I am sorry that I cannot provide a number.

Categories	Open-Ended Comments
Nothing to report; Takes issue with the survey; policy comments	I do believe that this is an important issue. But it is my opinion that Judges are the least likely to have knowledge of what happens after his/her case is closed.
Nothing to report	I do not recall receiving reports of harm or threats of harm experienced by any defendant, witness, or family or friends of a defendant or witness from cases on my docket in the past three years.
General comment about the frequency of harm; general comment about harm in prison/prison culture	I do not recall specifics but I do recall being informed (primarily in connection with sentencings that defendants have been threatened in detention facilities and/or their families threatened with physical harm in connection with actual or suspected cooperation. All in drug cases, some of which also involved charges of violent crime (including murder) against the person to whom the threats were attributed.
Nothing to report	I do not see any change in harm, threats, or worries about harm over the last three years (or over the last [redacted] years, for that matter). Clients are often worried about retaliation; however, I have never seen any evidence or stories about actual harm.
Details of a specific incident; Takes issue with the survey	I don't recall any cases involving witnesses being harmed or threatened before 2014. The harm experienced by a witness' family was a drive-by shooting of the family home allegedly arranged by one of the defendants.
General comment about the frequency of harm; Takes issue with the survey; general comments about the sources to identify cooperator	I got tired of answering the same way but I probably see 15 or so cases per year where a cooperating defendant in pretrial custody is [threatened] based on the knowledge he is cooperating based on debriefing statements placed in the [discovery] file of co-[conspirators].
Details of a specific incident; general comment about the frequency of harm	I had a multi-defendant case arising out of brutal assault of an expelled member of the [redacted]. All but one of the defendants pled. Three or four testified for the Government in the trial of the one defendant who went to trial. The "rule" of this [redacted] gang is that one does not get out of it alive. Those who testified were under threat of death, and one in particular — who had a prior State sentence to serve — sought (unsuccessfully) a deal to avoid having to serve his State term in the State prison for fear that he would be killed. The Assistant U.S. Attorney who led the initial prosecution was removed from handling further [redacted] cases at his request after he received death threats. / / Frequent death threats are made in illegal alien trafficking cases, to control the illegal aliens until transportation fees are collected, and occasionally some of these aliens are called as witnesses. / / An assistant U.S. Attorney and [I] are currently under death threats from a detained defendant awaiting sentencing on convictions including on one count of solicitation to commit a crime of violence.

Categories	Open-Ended Comments
Details of a specific incident	I had one cooperating witness who was concerned about potential threats once he was sentenced and started serving his custodial sentence. His main area of concern, however, centered around his deportation to [redacted] and the threat of harm facing him from drug cartels in [redacted].
Details of a specific incident	I have a large drug case involving about [redacted] defendants. Two of them claim that they were threatened not to cooperate.
Details of a specific incident	I have a pending case involving a local gang and allegations of 2 or more killings of cooperating witnesses.
Nothing to report	I have been a judge [redacted].
Nothing to report	I have been on senior status for [redacted] and have not had a criminal docket for the past three years.
Nothing to report	I have been on the bench less than [redacted].
Nothing to report	I have been on the bench less than [redacted].
Nothing to report	I have been on the bench only [redacted] and have had my criminal docket for only [about] [redacted]. I have am not aware of any threats thus far experienced by defendants and/or witnesses, or their family or friends.
Nothing to report	I have had counsel represent that there may be a potential threat of harm to a defendant or witness, however, I do not believe that there has been any actual harm or threat of harm. Or, maybe, I have just not been made aware.
Nothing to report	I have had no problems with threats of harm to clients or witnesses. If I ever had any issues, I am sure I could work with the government and the court to handle them on a case-specific basis.
Details of a specific incident; general comment about the frequency of harm	I have had one case in which a codefendant was murdered just before he was scheduled to appear for a change of plea. I have had other cases in which I learned that a witness was [threatened] but I cannot recall whether any of those instances occurred within the past three years.
Nothing to report	I have no information that any defendant or witness was harmed or threatened due to perceived or actual cooperation.
General comment about the frequency of harm; policy comments; general comments about the sources to identify cooperator	I have no other specific information to provide, but have the impression that the US Department of Justice and US Attorney's offices do not consider the protection of cooperating defendants (and to a lesser extent witnesses) to be much of a priority, despite the rapid increase in electronic access and search capabilities in recent years. Perhaps this is reflective of better information about the real threat to an incarcerated individual's relative safety, but fear there is a certain amount of fatalism (even cynicism) about what can be or should be to follow through on these protections. Instead, prosecutors seem to be defaulting on their telling the potential informant that, while efforts will be made to protect them, at the end of the day their safety cannot be assured.

Categories	Open-Ended Comments
Nothing to report	I have not been advised of any threats to anyone
Nothing to report; general comment about harm in prison/prison culture; general comment about the frequency of harm; general comments about the sources to identify cooperator; comments about refusal out of fear	I have not had any clients that, to my knowledge before or after, were threatened or harmed because of cooperation. I can tell you that the CW in jail is that other inmates at the FCI's they will be assigned to, will have access to their judgment and other docs and so will be able to tell if an inmate was granted a 5K or a reduced sentenced for cooperation and they fear retribution for that. The effect is to limit D.'s willing to cooperate. I have had a handful, maybe 6, cases in the past 3 years that the fear of retribution prevented their cooperation.
Nothing to report; general comment about the frequency of harm; general comment about harm in prison/prison culture; general comments about the sources to identify cooperator; comments about refusal out of fear	I have not had defendants/witnesses who have received actual threats or have been harmed because of cooperation or possible cooperation. However, it is common that defendants do not wish to have a cooperation provision in the plea agreement because of safety concerns. Those concerns are two-fold. One is the general concern about their family who will remain in the community. The other concern is that the paperwork at BOP will indicate they are cooperating. The fact that a defendant's cooperation is not kept secure by BOP is a major factor keeping many defendants from desiring to cooperate.
Nothing to report; general comments about the sources to identify cooperator; general comment about harm in prison/prison culture	I have not known of documents or transcripts to have been used. Typically it is the movement of the prisoner/witness in and out of the facility to meet with the AUSAs which enlighten fellow inmates.
Nothing to report	I have not received any information that defendants who are serving time after sentencing have been threatened in prison for cooperating.
Details of a specific incident	I have one case where the parties' attorneys have expressed serious concerns about any possible threats being made to the defendant during the cooperation period, especially because he is in custody.
Nothing to report	I have only been a District Judge for [redacted].
Nothing to report	I have only been a federal judge for [redacted]. During my tenure, I have not experienced harm/threats to witnesses or cooperators in any of my cases.
Nothing to report	I have only been a judge for [redacted].
Nothing to report	I have only been on the bench for [redacted].
Nothing to report	I have only been on the bench for [redacted].
General comment about the frequency of harm; general comment about harm in prison/prison culture; general comments about the sources to identify cooperator	I have only heard of threats to prisoners where their cooperation was discovered through reference to their plea agreements or 5K petition. I have no first hand knowledge of such activity in cases on my docket.
Nothing to report	I have only served as USDJ since [redacted] so I have a limited basis to compare.

Categories	Open-Ended Comments
Nothing to report	I have polled all current officers and supervisors and they do not recall [any] incidents within the past three years.
General comment about the frequency of harm; procedures for protecting defendants; general comment about harm in prison/prison culture; policy comments; general comments about the sources to identify cooperator	I have practiced actively in the [redacted] since [redacted]. Only one defendant (during the 90's) has been the subject of credible threats during a case and he was appropriately given a place to live outside of town by the FBI for a brief period. It is not infrequent that clients communicate from prison about cooperation allegations, including two or three times during the last three years. Clients have requested their PSR, docket sheet, phony letters from the US Attorney's office or from me. I am not aware of any client being the subject of actual harm. The current system of sealing cooperation agreements does not offer protection since plea agreements are public and anybody can do the math and compare guideline levels to actual sentences. Now that the Guidelines are discretionary, there is a risk of being falsely accused of being a cooperator if one gets a reduced sentence for some other reason. / / My view is that the only way to protect defendants is for less of the docket to be public records.
Details of a specific incident; Takes issue with the survey; general comment about the frequency of harm	I have presided over the [redacted] [trials] lasting [redacted]; The [redacted] that were [redacted]; subsequent subsets of [redacted] trials [redacted]; The [redacted] trials [redacted] and numerous other cases involving organized criminal gangs [redacted]. Cooperating witness and [witness] intimidation are standard and the present procedures highlight their cooperation and endanger witnesses. / I did not limit my comments the last three years. / [redacted]
Nothing to report	I just became a judge in [redacted] so I can't compare . . .
Nothing to report	I just took the bench on [redacted].
Details of a specific incident; general comments about the sources to identify cooperator	I know of only one case in the past three years. The case involved the exportation of military grade munitions. Once his cooperation was published in the local paper, his family in [redacted] asserted that they were compelled to move. His wife reported that [someone] shot into her vehicle, she added that her son was beaten up, and that they live in constant fear.
General comment about the frequency of harm	I learn from defense lawyers about threats. They learn about threats from [their] clients. Typically I do not learn of the details. I also am not told if the defendant requested protection. Lawyers are very reluctant to give much information about threats because sharing [details] may place their clients at further risk. I believe this is a problem that is under reported to the courts.
Nothing to report	I only became a judge in [redacted], so I have no basis for comparison.
Details of a specific incident; general comments about the sources to identify cooperator	I only recall one person who, when filing a 2255, requested it be sealed due to fears of threats as he had been a cooperating defendant.

Categories	Open-Ended Comments
Details of a specific incident; general comments about the sources to identify cooperator	I recall one case where I was informed that a cooperating witness was subjected to threats, including on the internet, for participating in the trial
Details of a specific incident; general comments about the sources to identify cooperator	I recall only the one case I have previously described and the Motion to Vacate at issue and the opinion were issued in 2014 but defendant's allegation of being [harassed] by inmates based on the opinion were raised in 2015
Details of a specific incident; general comments about the sources to identify cooperator	I recently sentenced a defendant who had from jail instructed his girlfriend to identify a co-conspirator on rats.com for cooperating.
Procedures for protecting defendants	I require all documents that reference cooperation or potential cooperation to be filed under seal. I also seal transcripts. I have sealed or moved sentencing hearings.
Nothing to report; Takes issue with the survey; general comment about the frequency of harm	I spoke with [redacted] and was told if i did not recall a specific number I should respond with the number "0", which I have done. / / Also this survey is too absolute in its questioning. A whole host of factors may go into the client's decision to cooperate or not, not only the fear of harm or retaliation. So any cause and effect analysis is misleading. Suffice it to say that fear is present in almost any drug case where there is cooperation.
Details of a specific incident	I took the oath in [redacted], so I have a limited data set from which to answer. / / The one case I described, where a shot was taken aimed at an informant, (which missed), is the only incident with which I am familiar.
General comment about harm in prison/prison culture; general comment about the frequency of harm; details of a specific incident	I tried to indicate that every client who is sent to BOP requests their "paperwork" to prove they are not a cooperator. The number is much higher than I indicated but the survey did not accept the number I put in so I dropped it to 10. A client has two weeks to produce their documents once they enter BOP to prove they are not a cooperator otherwise they are subjected to physical harm. One client was beat senseless with a lock in a sock, he suffered severe head wounds. They are all threatened once they arrive in BOP custody.
General comment about the frequency of harm; policy comments	I understand that the only way generally for a defendant to receive a departure, is to cooperate, the extension of that cooperation can not only lead to a dangerous situation for the defendant, but also for the officer supervising that defendant. It is critical that the AUSA and the agents advise officers of a defendant's cooperation, so that they are not put in an unnecessary high risk situation.
Nothing to report	I was confirmed in [redacted], so I am unable to make a comparison between 2013 and 2014.
Details of a specific incident; comments about refusal out of fear	I was dealing with defendants associated with the [redacted] drug cartel. Cooperators and their family members were under constant threat. Numerous defendants refused to protect their family members in [redacted].
Nothing to report	I was not on the bench in [redacted].

Categories	Open-Ended Comments
Nothing to report	I was off of our criminal law draw for most of the past three years. I went on the draw for about three months in about [redacted], and drew three long cases and, therefore, took myself out of the criminal draw again. The trials were [redacted] weeks, respectively. So, I probably have little to add to this survey.
Nothing to report	I was sworn in on [redacted], so my experience is very limited.
Nothing to report	I would not have information about this because it is not a matter ordinarily brought to my attention.
General comment about the frequency of harm; comments about refusal out of fear	I wrote 15 for the number for people who withdrew. It is likely higher. We are in [redacted] where many of our clients are so fearful, b/c of the environment, that we can't even get clients to have a safety valve interview. Clients would rather do their mandatory minimum than be labeled a "snitch." Dozens and dozens of our clients refuse to cooperate out of fear and the threats.
General comments about the sources to identify cooperator	if there are sealed pleading on the docket sheet, the assumption is that client is cooperating
Nothing to report	I'm a new judge and therefore do not have relevant information.
General comment about the frequency of harm; policy comments	I'm afraid my lack of recollection does not allow me to recount the many more instances over the [redacted] years I have been on the bench in which cooperating defendants have been afraid after they have provided information. My experience is that there is a complete disconnect between the United States Attorneys Office and the Bureau of Prisons such that once a defendant is no longer needed, he is discarded and the interest and knowledge in how best to protecting him or her is minimal to non-existent. There is no sense of commitment to the safety of the cooperator for the duration of his term in custody or upon release.
Details of a specific incident; general comment about the frequency of harm	In a large drug trafficking case, a witness/cooperator received a threat via letter. The letter was sent to the witnesses/defendant's family. The FBI is investigating the case. Often, in other cases, many defendants allege that they will be harmed for cooperating - however it's difficult to verify if any actual harm might befall them.
Details of a specific incident; general comment about the frequency of harm; general comments about the sources to identify cooperator	In approximately 2010 there was a huge upsurge in drug conspiracy cases involving violence. Two of the cases that I make reference to in this survey involved RICO drug conspiracies. One of the cases was a RICO drug conspiracy involving a [redacted] gang. It was through trial testimony that I learned of the extensive use of court documents (particularly PreSentence Investigation Reports and Plea Agreements) in prison to identify cooperators.

Categories	Open-Ended Comments
Procedures for protecting defendants	In coordination with the District Court, we have implemented a procedure to keep cooperation provisions of plea agreements under seal. Standard non-cooperation plea agreements are filed and appear on PACER. Cooperation provisions in all cases are contained in Supplemental Plea Agreements which are filed under seal using a single Magistrate (MJ) case number.
Procedures for protecting defendants; general comment about the frequency of harm; details of a specific incident	In every 5K motion there is a section about potential harm — most of the time the government says there are no known threats but that given the cooperation threats are a possibility — my experience has been that they disclose the threats orally at sidebar at sentencing, because they don't want to write the details down, so we don't have records and my memory is not great about individual cases. The most blatant example I had involved a [redacted] store selling T-shirts with the cooperator's photo and the words "[cooperator's name] is a snitch" — but the knowledge did not come from court, people learned of it during the investigative stage.
Details of a specific incident; general comments about the sources to identify cooperator	In [redacted], the defendant on supervised release in my case testified before a federal grand jury in an unrelated matter. He was murdered in [redacted] in [redacted]. It appears that the defendants in the unrelated matter found out about his grand jury testimony.
Procedures for protecting defendants	In multiple Defendant drug cases where a Defendant has cooperated, I am seeing situations where the defense attorney and prosecutor schedule a meeting with me to explain the Defendant is cooperating; however, because of safety concerns for the defendant and his family members, they do not want the docket to reflect any notations to a sealed proceeding. Instead of the U.S. filing a sealed 5k motion, there is a Rule 11(c)(1)(C) plea agreement to a specific sentence or to a specific range and the joint request by defense counsel and the prosecutor is to accept the plea agreement without making any reference on the record to the defendant's cooperation for personal safety reasons. / / My clear preference would be for a sealed 5k motion for downward departure for substantial assistance; however, I have agreed to the off the record procedure requested by defense counsel and the prosecutor because I do not want to see any harm come to the defendant and/or his or her family members.
General comment about harm in prison/prison culture; general comment about the frequency of harm	In my cases, many of my clients have contacted me to obtain transcripts of their sentencing hearings, or copies of the dockets in their cases so that they can show other inmates that they did not cooperate. They have told me that other inmates require this information so that they can prove that they are not "snitches."

Categories	Open-Ended Comments
Details of a specific incident; general comments about the sources to identify cooperator	In one case prosecuted recently, the informant /witness was threatened after the defendant's family posted the tapes of the undercover buys the informant made on YouTube. The tapes had been provided to the public defender as discovery. The public defender turned these over to the defendant's family, and subsequently, the family posted the videos on-line. The office has addressed this problem with the public defender to ensure that such an episode will not be repeated.
Details of a specific incident; general comments about the sources to identify cooperator; general comment about harm in prison/prison culture; procedures for protecting defendants	In one case, the defendant was involved with members of violent known street gangs, such as [redacted], but who also would engage in unaffiliated acts of violence for hire in connection with their drug trafficking activities. The defendant used information obtained pursuant to the Jencks Act to ascertain the identities of potential witnesses, some of whom were incarcerated, some of whom had pled guilty but were at liberty (of these some received veiled threats not to testify and one was assaulted- presumably in connection with his anticipated testimony). This defendant also tried to provide economic assistance to one cooperator to buy his silence by providing commissary money and providing money to his family. / / In the third case, the defendants involved in assaulting a perceived cooperator were members of a violent ethnic criminal group. The assault occurred without any concrete proof that the alleged cooperator was, in fact, cooperating on their case. In fact, the person was not providing information on their case. The assault was videotaped in the federal jail facility. Additional comments provided via email: There are certain circumstances that may serve as signs to defendants or persons trying to identify who is cooperating with the government in a criminal case or ongoing investigation. For example, --- If the person has pled guilty and the sentence has been held in abeyance for any unusual length of time, usually more than 3 or 4 months. --- If the person pled guilty to a prosecutor's information as opposed to an indictment before there was an indictment filed. --- Because incarcerated defendants who have been convicted by guilty plea (or sometimes trial) are pressured by other inmates to obtain a copy of their presentence report to prove they are not cooperators, our district's Probation Department no longer mentions the defendant's cooperation with the government or the possibility of a 5K1.1 motion as a possible departure factor in the presentence reports. Any cooperation is addressed in the sentence recommendation, which is not sent to the prison officials, and is submitted to the court separately from the presentence report.

Categories	Open-Ended Comments
Details of a specific incident; general comment about harm in prison/prison culture	In one instance, a defendant attempted to recruit an inmate incarcerated with the co-defendant cooperator to harm the cooperator. In another instance, a spouse of a co-defendant (who was also a defendant) in a drug conspiracy case was raped by members of a gang involved in the conspiracy because she agreed to cooperate with the government.
Details of a specific incident; comments about refusal out of fear	In one of the cases on which I worked as a magistrate judge, a confidential informant was murdered the day after agents arrested a number of participants in a drug conspiracy. In another case involving multiple defendants who were involved in a drug conspiracy, one of the [redacted] defendants who was a minor player in the conspiracy but who had information about at least one of the leaders of the conspiracy, declined an opportunity to cooperate with the Government out of concern for his family. In that case, we learned that another member of the conspiracy was paying the defendant's attorney fees and was participating in decisions about the defense provided to the defendant. I removed the defense attorney and appointed new counsel for the defendant.
Procedures for protecting defendants; general comment about harm in prison/prison culture	In our Court [redacted] we have local rules that allow the sealing of such documents as Motions for 5Ki.i and 3553 relief, Sentencing memorandum, Guilty Plea Memos and Agreements when cooperation of the pleading defendant is at issue. We cannot (and I would not) seal an entire case file, but orders to seal enough documents in a case will be revealing on the docket to those assisting a defendant target. Pre-sentence Investigation reports should not cite cooperation of any defendant, either. / Separating the cooperator(s) in a particular case who are all housed [in] the same facility is also a challenge, but the effort must be made by the prosecutors as well as the FDC and BOP.
Procedures for protecting defendants	In our district, all sentencing memoranda, 5K motions, and plea agreement cooperation agreements are sealed by default. I believe this has been very effective in controlling the effect on cooperating defendants and witnesses.

Categories	Open-Ended Comments
General comment about the frequency of harm; procedures for protecting defendants; general comments about the sources to identify cooperator	In the [redacted], the United States Attorney's Office ("USAO") prosecutes a number of cases annually charging defendants who are members of violent street gangs, organized crime groups, and large-scale drug trafficking organizations. One of the central tenants of many of these organizations is that those who cooperate with law enforcement against these organizations are automatically targeted for murder or some other form of physical harm. As a result, it is not at all unusual for cooperating defendants and cooperating witnesses to receive threats directed by the criminal groups they are cooperating against. (Although, chiefly as a result of the great care that is typically taken to protect cooperating witnesses and defendants from harm, it is rare for these threats to materialize into actual harm that befalls these individuals.) / / As a result of the nature of the threat faced by cooperating witnesses and defendants who cooperating against some of the violent criminal organizations prosecuted in the [redacted], the USAO routinely seeks permission to file under seal with the court pleadings -- such as sentencing memoranda and plea agreements -- that disclose the fact a defendant or witness is cooperating with the government; and district courts in the [redacted] regularly provide authorization for the government to file such pleadings under seal. While this may provide some measure of protection for individuals who cooperate with the government, it is not a fool-proof method of concealing an individual's cooperation from those who may want to do him or her harm, as the fact that such a pleading has been filed under seal may alone signal to a member of one of these groups that a particular individual is cooperating and these groups often need only to speculate that an individual is cooperating before seeking to do him or her harm.
General comment about the frequency of harm	In the [redacted], we have a large percentage of defendants who cooperate with the government. The majority of threats are coming from drug cartel members who reside in [redacted] and travel back and forth across the border. Most of the defendants who report the threats state they have been kidnapped, beaten, and threatened by the cartel. The threats usually extend to the defendant's family members as well.

Categories	Open-Ended Comments
General comment about the frequency of harm; general comments about the sources to identify cooperator	In the vast majority of the cases, rumors led to threats of harm or assault. However, the co-defendant or unindicted co-conspirator had no proof that the defendant was actually cooperating.
General comments about the sources to identify cooperator; details of a specific incident; procedures for protecting defendants	In this district both plea agreements outline the government's intent to request a sentence reduction for cooperation and the Statement of Reasons is still considered by the Court as a public document and thus is available with the judgment on CM/ECF. / / Of the two offenders threatened while on supervised release -- one we made arrangements to transfer supervision to another district and the other one is currently in process of attempting a transfer. The current one being threatened was sentenced in a different district.
Procedures for protecting defendants; nothing to report; policy comments	In this district we have very few threats of harm. We believe taking actions to seal information for a minority of persons for the explicit reason of making the information more difficult to obtain, will harm the majority of our clients by making otherwise public information secret and by depriving them of potentially exculpatory or mitigating information (what agreements other similarly situated persons have obtained, how to compare others convicted of the same offense, etc.). We strongly oppose this idea for those reasons. In addition, some courts of appeals look unfavorably on sealing any documents and have strict rules as to when and how documents can be sealed.
Details of a specific incident; general comment about harm in prison/prison culture; general comments about the sources to identify cooperator	In [redacted], the defendant [redacted] was a local rap artist in [redacted]. [redacted] compiled and released a rap video on YouTube that identified (by name) government cooperators. The government was successful in having the video removed from YouTube. This occurred in [redacted]. On a separate matter, we have received information in the past that inmates in BOP custody were being required to provide other inmates with a copy of their presentence report in order to confirm that they were not cooperating with the government. No specific case references are [available].

Categories	Open-Ended Comments
Details of a specific incident; general comments about the sources to identify cooperator; procedures for protecting defendants; procedures for protecting juries	In [redacted], the government arrested [redacted] people involved with a very violent drug conspiracy known as [redacted]. Most of those arrested were held at the Federal Detention Center, and although there were separation orders, the A.U.S.A. reported to the Court a large number of threats made by the organization leaders [redacted]. The organization took the position that even a defendant's guilty plea qualified as cooperation, even if that defendant provided no further assistance against other co-defendants. The Court broke the organization up into three groups for trial and tried four individuals in the first of the three groups, resulting in convictions for all four. The Court ordered an anonymous jury and the U.S. Marshals escorted jurors to and from the juror parking lot from undisclosed locations. None of the defendants has cooperated against his or her co-defendants, though some have pleaded guilty. Those who have pleaded guilty have made clear that they are putting in a plea for themselves only, not agreeing to cooperate against any of their co-defendants.
General comments about the sources to identify cooperator	It appears most harm was done by people who knew them previously, not [through] court documents or information made public through judicial means.
General comment about the frequency of harm; general comments about the sources to identify cooperator	It appears that more uncharged witnesses (not defendant-witnesses) are threatened, than defendants. Additionally, it appears that frequently, at least at the earlier stages of the cases, the witnesses are identified through conclusions drawn from discovery (even if redacted to protect identity for a time). Additionally, in many cases there are not actual threats, but an expressed fear by the defendant of cooperating due to concern for self or family. Many such defendants express concern through their counsel about the sealing of the cooperation agreement and how it appears on the court's docket (such as whether there is a missing number on the docket).
General comment about the frequency of harm; general comment about harm in prison/prison culture	It is a recurrent theme. I could have continued to answer yes over and over again in this survey. I often read it in PSR where the officer states that the defendant and/or his family was threatened when they learned or suspected that he was cooperating. So I really wasn't thinking of one specific case but of many. Everyone seems to find out in jail about who is a snitch!

Categories	Open-Ended Comments
Takes issue with the survey; procedures for protecting defendants; general comments about the sources to identify cooperator; general comment about the frequency of harm	It is almost impossible to know the exact number of witnesses or defendants who have been threatened from information learned or acquired from PACER. In our district, plea supplements contain the information about cooperation and the potential for downward departures. They are filed under seal. However, one can see that there is a sealed document by the fact that a numbered document is [missing]. Likewise, 5K1.1 motions are filed under seal. However, again the missing document number and the proximity to sentencing is a give away. The same is true for Rule 35 motions, filed under seal with a missing number and shortly thereafter an Amended [Judgment] is filed. Furthermore, witnesses and cooperating defendants, when threatened, generally do not know how the assailant learned of their cooperation.
Policy comments	It is essential that we develop and implement on a national basis uniform procedures and practices to reduce or eliminate the risk of harm to cooperators arising out of public access to court records. My district, [redacted], has developed procedures to do so, but these will be of little effect unless [these] procedures, or something similar to them, are adopted throughout the country.
General comment about the frequency of harm; general comment about harm in prison/prison culture; procedures for protecting defendants; policy comments	It is increasingly true that defendant's worry they will be asked, either during pre-trial incarceration or once placed in the Bureau of Prisons, for their plea paperwork to see if they have cooperated. Refusing to provide it is considered proof of cooperation. I have had a court allow me to submit the plea paperwork with a cryptic reference to a sealed document outlining the cooperation and its 5K benefits. We definitely need a way to help [defendants] who cooperate from being put in this predicament.
General comment about the frequency of harm; general comment about harm in prison/prison culture; general comments about the sources to identify cooperator	It is now regular BOP inmate practice to demand "papers" to determine whether another provided cooperation and assistance to the government, or is a convicted sex offender where minors were involved. Inmates regularly request copies of their docketing statement, judgment and commitment order, and statement of reasons section.
Nothing to report	I've been in this position for less than a year, so my perspective on the questions is very limited.
Details of a specific incident; procedures for protecting defendants; general comments about the sources to identify cooperator	I've [only] been on the bench [redacted]...so not a lot of context to respond. I had one case where the potential for 5K1.1 was mentioned in the plea agreement. Later, the FPD asked permission to substitute a revised plea agreement (so it would appear as the "original" [agreement] on the docket), deleting reference to cooperation because of threats conveyed to defendant's family. My clerk has also reported anecdotal instances of "rough and [suspicious]" looking people coming to the [public] viewing terminal to see plea agreements and/or 5K motions.

Categories	Open-Ended Comments
Details of a specific incident; general comments about the sources to identify cooperator	Just the one incident mentioned earlier. It occurred in a multi-defendant drug case. The witness was a defendant in a related multi-defendant drug case and was seen coming back from court. Unclear how one of the defendants (the one who threatened him) knew he had cooperated.
General comment about harm in prison/prison culture; general comment about the frequency of harm	Many clients who were sentenced to a BOP facility have requested court documents that confirm that they were not cooperators.
General comment about harm in prison/prison culture; general comment about the frequency of harm; procedures for protecting defendants; comments about refusal out of fear	Many of our clients request their paperwork after they report to BOP and tell us that if they do not prove they were not cooperating they will be in physical danger. In our district we routinely seal matters on the docket and close hearings that are related to cooperation. We do not track numbers - but we often have witnesses refuse to be interviewed by us in fear that cooperation will tag them as a "snitch" and place them in physical danger.
General comment about the frequency of harm	Many of the threats were made by the defendants appearing before me of actual and potential witnesses against them. I have seen correspondence and transcripts of phone calls containing such threats.
Procedures for protecting witnesses	Many of those [threatened] went into witness protection.
General comment about harm in prison/prison culture; general comment about the frequency of harm	Many requests for transcripts because of demands from other inmates in prison to prove that the defendant was not a cooperator. Some threats to defendants whose sentencing hearings have been postponed when co-defendant trials are postponed because they are assumed to be cooperating.
Comments about refusal out of fear; general comment about harm in prison/prison culture; general comment about the frequency of harm; general comments about the sources to identify cooperator	Many times defendants will refuse to cooperate because of threats to family, friends or themselves. There is also the fear of the unknown when they reach BOP, as it is common knowledge that "cooperators" are targeted. Further, all of our plea agreements contain boilerplate language regarding cooperation, so anyone in this district could be identified as a cooperator even when they did not cooperate. We also receive many variances on factors other than cooperation, and defendants are concerned that the variances, though not related to cooperation, may target them in prison. We routinely give a copy of the sentencing memorandum we prepare to clients. 5K motions prepared by the government are not shared with us.
General comment about the frequency of harm	Most cases involved illegal aliens with ties to drug cartels in [redacted]. Defendants feared for their [families'] safety. Whether actual threats or simply fear arising out of the retributive reputations of the cartels was the cause of reluctance to provide information, I cannot say.
Procedures for protecting defendants; general comments about the sources to identify cooperator	Most information is anecdotal. No hard details are available. It is our practice to seal any filing or proceeding that references cooperators, except the testimony of a cooperator in open court.

Categories	Open-Ended Comments
General comment about the frequency of harm; general comments about the sources to identify cooperator	Most of the cases involve individuals in either pretrial detention or release status who were threatened by individuals (often co-defendants) who knew the "victims" were assisting the government either after arrest, or had cooperated with law enforcement prior to arrest. I believe very little of the information about cooperators was gleaned through court documents, mostly it was by word of mouth or from the street.
General comment about the frequency of harm; details of a specific incident	Most of the cases where I have clients who reported threats of harm arise in in drug conspiracy cases, mostly involving [redacted]. The reported threats have been both implied and explicit. The implied threats typically involve someone telling the defendant they know where he lives or where his family lives. One [explicit] threat involved discussions as to whether to cut the defendant's fingers off or kill him.
General comment about the frequency of harm; general comments about the sources to identify cooperator	Most of the problems our clients face are because of the nature of their charges, eg child pornography cases. Those clients are very concerned about the privacy of their court files and records.
General comments about the sources to identify cooperator; nothing to report	Most of the threats came as a result of actual trial testimony by the defendants/offenders who were threatened. I have no information in any of the cases that points to court documents being used to identify the defendants/offenders as cooperators.
General comment about the frequency of harm; procedures for protecting defendants	Most requests to seal cases have been due to the protection of the ability of a defendant to cooperate without the possible targets learning of the Defendant's agreement to cooperate which would impede the Defendant's ability to lure into traps the government has devised for the cooperation. I have not heard of any person who was a witness to a case to whom a threat was made.
Comments about refusal out of fear; general comment about harm in prison/prison culture	Mostly gang defendants and witnesses don't want to cooperate because of actual or perceived harm and the need to prove they are not cooperators by sufficient documentation when they enter the bureau of prisons
Details of a specific incident	my client that was harmed was attacked while in transit--he was threatened several other times, also while being transported to/from court or facilities
General comment about the frequency of harm; comments about refusal out of fear	My clients are concerned about harm to themselves or family in cooperation cases but I have not had any clients decline to cooperate for that reason.
Nothing to report	My judgeship began in [redacted].

Categories	Open-Ended Comments
General comment about the frequency of harm; general comment about harm in prison/prison culture; general comments about the sources to identify cooperator	My [only] [information] about possible harm to witnesses comes from occasional comments by agents or AUSAs that detained defendants have been "reaching out" to persons outside the jail to have them, in turn, contact persons believed to be [cooperators]. I don't know how often this happens, but assume that it's not uncommon. AUSAs & USMS Deputies would be better sources of data. / / I do know that prison inmates are being called on to get and provide to others copies of their PSRs and, perhaps, transcripts of sentencings. Docket sheets containing sealed plea agreements or sentencing [memoranda] area big red flag.
Takes issue with the survey	My responses to the two previous questions left blank is: fewer than 10.
Nothing to report	N.A.
Nothing to report	N/A
Nothing to report	N/A
Nothing to report	N/A
Nothing to report	N/A
Nothing to report	N/A
Nothing to report	n/a
Nothing to report; procedures for protecting defendants	Neither my staff nor I can remember any instance in the past three years of defendants or witnesses being harmed or threatened because of that person's cooperation with the government. In fact, I can't remember any such instance in my [redacted] on the bench. / I know we are careful in my jurisdiction to seal sentencing memos and transcripts of sentencing hearings whenever cooperation is involved or at least whenever I am requested to do so by defense counsel or the government. It is also, of course, possible that we just haven't heard of harms or threats that occur after our cases are closed but I am [sensitive] on the subject and would remember if it had come to my attention.
Takes issue with the survey; general comment about the frequency of harm; comments about refusal out of fear; procedures for protecting witnesses	Neither the USAO nor law enforcement agencies track this data, so we have been compelled to provide estimates. Further, it is not clear what the survey means by a witness "withdrawing an offer of cooperation" as opposed to "refusing cooperation." Witnesses, especially in drug and violent crime cases, frequently live in urban areas where "snitching" carries enormous danger. Law enforcement agents commonly hit a wall of silence in a community, stemming largely from the fear that powerful groups will kill witnesses who are seen as providing information to the government. Frequently, this wall of silence can be penetrated only if we manage to arrest and detain many members of the group, freeing residents of fear of retaliation.

Categories	Open-Ended Comments
Nothing to report; procedures for protecting defendants; general comments about the sources to identify cooperator	No client has reported harm or threats of harm in the last three (3) years. Requests for docket info have decreased since the [redacted] has instituted a policy of sealing ALL plea agreements, not just those entitled Plea and Cooperation Agreements. Those who have asked in the last three (3) years do not report harm or threats of harm in their requests as those requests are probably being screened by those threatening/doing the harm, but that cannot be verified.
Nothing to report	No harm or threats occurred.
Nothing to report	No incidents.
Nothing to report	no threats occurred to my knowledge
Nothing to report	No threats or harm that I am aware of
Nothing to report	No threats, thus no change.
Nothing to report	None
Nothing to report	None known.
Nothing to report	None of my cases that I supervised have experienced threats or harm.
Details of a specific incident; comments about refusal out of fear	None of my clients were actually harmed. I had one defendant whose family in another country was threatened. He refused to cooperate.
Nothing to report	None of these matters have been brought to my attention.
Nothing to report	None that I can recall, after checking with my Courtroom Deputy and my Probation Officer liaison.
Nothing to report	None that I know of.
Nothing to report	not applicable
Nothing to report	not applicable, because [I'm] not aware of any such threat to a witness or defendant in any of my cases.
Nothing to report	Not aware of any harm or threat of harm
Nothing to report	Not sure this is a real issue in our district.
General comment about the frequency of harm; policy comments; takes issue with the survey; comments about refusal out of fear	Obviously, gang and prison inmate prosecution create the greatest threat of actual violence and potential for frightening witnesses from testifying. While "transparency" is at the bedrock of our judicial system, with gang, organized crime, and prison prosecutions transparency comes at a high price when cooperators are an integral part of the prosecution or investigation. Questions 2 and 4 require a highly speculative response. My experience shows that a large number of potential witnesses and defendants are [deterred] and therefore refuse to cooperate because they perceive danger to themselves or their families. I would [not] know if they didn't tell me or refuse an offer, so, my quantification of the numbers is speculative.

Categories	Open-Ended Comments
Details of a specific incident; procedures for protecting defendants	On the first defendant, that individual was placed in protective custody after being harmed/shot. / With respect to the second defendant, that individual was housed in protective custody in a hotel. / With respect to the third defendant, that individual had physical harm but declined any protective custody.
Details of a specific incident; procedures for protecting defendants	One additional threat to report (can't go back in survey). Offender on supervised release, cooperated against fellow gang members, separated while in custody and USPO work to keep him separate during supervision activities. Threat was actual physical harm.
Details of a specific incident; procedures for protecting defendants	One case in which a defendant on TSR was murdered after [testifying] in court (gang related) and another case were we had to transfer or move a pretrial defendant to another district.
Details of a specific incident; general comment about the frequency of harm; general comment about harm in prison/prison culture; procedures for protecting defendants; comments about refusal out of fear	One client got [his] face slashed in as a result of his cooperation. Numerous clients request information in order to show they did not cooperate. This number includes clients who did cooperate, but who may not have received a sentence reduction or whose plea agreement did not contain cooperation language. These clients believe they will be harmed if other inmates believe or find out the client cooperated. Two clients requested having solitary confinement protection because they could not provide the ECF docket report to other inmates, since the ECF docket report would show a reduction for cooperating with the government. No one recalls any instances where witnesses were threatened. Third party cooperators have backed out due to perceived danger.
Details of a specific incident; procedures for protecting defendants	one client had to be placed in the BOP witness protection program due to the severity of the threats against him by other BOP inmates.
Details of a specific incident; comments about refusal out of fear; general comment about the frequency of harm; general comment about harm in prison/prison culture	One client knew of a witness murdered in [redacted]. He flatly refused to cooperate. He received life after conviction at trial. I have many clients who ask for 'fake' documents. One client was beaten while in prison and did lengthy time in segregation. This problem has increased much in last 2 years. Not sure why.
Details of a specific incident; Takes issue with the survey	One defendant was charged with witness intimidation. Also, I assume the survey includes the gov't threatening witnesses with charges or perjury, misprision, and/or conspiracy.
Details of a specific incident	One instance of a threat to family members. This was addressed by both counsel. If my docket is any example, threats and harm do not appear to be a significant problem in this district.
Details of a specific incident	One of the cases was actively cooperating. The other case involved co-defendants who had been boyfriend/girlfriend and were both out on release.

Categories	Open-Ended Comments
General comment about harm in prison/prison culture; comments about refusal out of fear; general comments about the sources to identify cooperator	One of the main concerns regarding defendants /offenders in our district is the safety valve requirement. Once in custody and after they plea, [an] inmate has to demonstrate to other inmates that he/she is not cooperating with the government. As proof of this, they have to show their plea agreement and [often] they are not willing to comply with the safety valve for fear of retaliation
Details of a specific incident; procedures for protecting defendants	One offender was victimized twice by [redacted] gang members in [redacted]. He was placed in a hotel for 30 days for safety and relocated to [redacted].
Procedures for protecting witnesses; details of a specific incident	One witness was placed in the WITSEC program after cooperating. Testimony was not needed because all defendants pleaded guilty. The witness was not a successful participant in the programs due to rule violations.
General comment about the frequency of harm; policy comments; procedures for protecting defendants	Other than a general concern about a possible threat, I am unaware of a specific threat or attacks made to a specific defendant /witness, and I have handled a fairly heavy criminal docket involving "drugs and guns" for years. AUSAs have also mentioned to me that until recently there was no reason for alarm, but all of a sudden there is a big push either by defense lawyers and/or DOJ to have everything sealed for 35b's or 5k1s. This is despite that there is not one documented incident that I am aware of in all the cases that I have handled of a problem. Many are advocating sealing everything of a cooperative nature now but this is in my opinion inconsistent with any empirical evidence that i am aware of and the first amendment right of the public to know about court proceedings and filings. / / /
General comment about the frequency of harm; procedures for protecting defendants	Our district has had numerous [redacted] cases and security is usually increased during trials/sentencings because of rumors of threats. I have very limited information regarding those threats or rumors.
Procedures for protecting defendants; general comment about the frequency of harm; general comments about the sources to identify cooperator	Our practices have changed in recent years to make docket and in court references more oblique and less suggestive of cooperation. Often we [refrain] from discuss[ing] 5K1 documents and we [camouflage] them on the docket. We have been informed with increasing frequency that codefendants purchase transcripts of hearings regarding an alleged cooperating defendant and/or witness and manage to access electronic dockets with help from others on the outside. These procedures require some careful management by the judge and others involved in the process.
General comment about the frequency of harm	Please keep in mind that my courthouse sits [redacted]. I hear from hundreds of defendants that they were threatened and/or harmed in [redacted] immediately prior their offenses in the [redacted]. For those who believe that narcotics traffickers are not dangerous criminals need to come sit in my court and hear/see the real stories of what happens in [redacted] by such traffickers.

Categories	Open-Ended Comments
Nothing to report	Please note that my statistical sample is quite small, in that I am a relatively new judge ([redacted] on the bench).
General comment about the frequency of harm	Primarily I recall threats against AUSAs and/or one defense or public defender.
General comment about harm in prison/prison culture	Prison gangs are an on-going problem.
General comment about the frequency of harm	Reported threats typically are brought to the court's [attention] by defense attorneys during the sentencing hearing, and mostly pertain to families outside the United States in drug trafficking cases. I am unaware of any reported threats being carried out.
General comment about the frequency of harm; details of a specific incident	Reports of threats against cooperating defendants are routine in this district. Actual harm is more rare, but it occurs. I have been personally involved in two cases in [redacted] in which witnesses were murdered.
General comment about harm in prison/prison culture; procedures for protecting defendants	Seems to me the real problem is what occurs after the cooperators begin serving a prison sentence. It is there that fellow prisoners request "proof" that the individual did not cooperate. It's there, too, where some have to seek refuge in the SHU. At least in my experience, it isn't that big of a problem pretrial.
General comment about the frequency of harm; general comments about the sources to identify cooperator	Some cooperators are so fearful that they do not want to receive 5K1.1 reductions to their sentences, nor do they want any mention of cooperation in court records or in court proceedings. In some instances, defendants who have not cooperated, or those who did cooperate but did not want a sentence reduction, request copies of the sentencing transcript and presentence report so that they can "prove" that did not cooperate.
General comment about the frequency of harm; general comments about the sources to identify cooperator; procedures for protecting defendants	Some of the threats were vague in my opinion. I only recall one case with specificity, but believe the frequency of the issue has not increased in the last year. Frankly, when a motion is filed by the government under seal at or about the time of the defendant's sentencing-- if it is identified as a motion filed by the government, a reader of the docket could [easily] surmise the sealed motion is a 5K1.1. I am unsure but believe the "sealed motions" are now listed as sealed documents and the filer is not identified. This is how it should be.
Details of a specific incident	The answers to the questions on this page are [estimates] based on conversations with prosecutors in our office.

Categories	Open-Ended Comments
Procedures for protecting defendants; policy comments	The better prosecutors and criminal defense bar have become much more sophisticated in keeping documentation reflecting cooperation by third party witnesses as well as defendants out of the public eye- i.e. no initial formal arrest paper work and/or bond allowing the defendant to cooperate fully prior to being formally charged which in many instances is driven by a post-cooperation negotiated plea to a particular offense that is actually capped in terms of available sentencing options- such as the 48 month maximum sentence for use of the telephone in a drug conspiracy. In other instances plea agreements are negotiated on the basis of specific relevant conduct that may defacto serve to cap the sentence without the Court necessarily having to formally become involved with the matter of the defendant's cooperation. / / Finally, given the fact that the sentencing guidelines are advisory, along with today's more infrequent use of the 21 U.S.C. 851 enhancement, there are more cases being processed without the Court ever having to address the subject of a reduced sentence under U.S.S.G. 5K1.1 or Rule 35(b). / / All of that said, there will never be a perfect solution to the dilemmas faced by defendants, witnesses, prosecutors, defense attorneys, as well we, as judges. All we might do collectively is to reduce where possible the wrong people learning about who is or has been a cooperating defendant or witness. Truly, the long-standing practice of sealing documents as well as formal sentencing hearings has not served the laudatory goal of providing anything close to a measure of protection for cooperating defendants. /
Details of a specific incident; general comments about the sources to identify cooperator; general comment about the frequency of harm	The case I described earlier in this survey was one in which, if I recall correctly, a warrant was not sealed and retaliation was either threatened or likely. I am aware of other anecdotal instances in which prosecutors and defense attorneys have felt retaliation was likely, but I am not aware of any details. Often these instances are revealed when a prosecutor or defense attorney asks during sentencing to disclose cooperation information at the bench.
Details of a specific incident; general comments about the sources to identify cooperator	The case [referenced] was [redacted], in which [redacted], a member of [redacted], learned that another member of [redacted], [redacted], was quoted in [redacted] presentence report as identifying [redacted] as a made member of the [redacted]. The page from the presentence report was shown to [redacted], [redacted], who ordered a hit--the murder--of [redacted]. [redacted] was convicted of the murder at trial.

Categories	Open-Ended Comments
General comment about the frequency of harm; general comment about harm in prison/prison culture; procedures for protecting defendants	The [climate] is worsening for everyone, cooperators and non-cooperators, especially in prison. It is reported by clients in our District and nationwide that when you arrive in prison you are given a certain length of time to prove through your documents that you are not a snitch. Without such proof, you are not allowed safe access to the prison yard. If you can't prove that you are not a snitch you end up in segregation or bouncing from prison to prison or worse.
General comment about harm in prison/prison culture; general comments about the sources to identify cooperator; general comment about the frequency of harm	The consistent theme that we have heard about regarding defendants or offenders in our District, is incarcerated offenders being coerced or threatened while in BOP custody or RRC facility (pre-release) if they did not try to get a copy of their presentence investigation, or plea agreement and provide it to the threatening party. The threatening party is usually doing this to ascertain whether an offender has been a cooperating witness or received a sentence reduction for cooperation (snitching) to government officials.
Details of a specific incident; general comments about the sources to identify cooperator; general comment about harm in prison/prison culture; procedures for protecting defendants	The Defendant in question not only made a deal with the Government, he actually testified at a jury trial against the other two defendants. There was no question but that his file contained plea deal specifics, and that the co defendants knew what the deal was (it was brought out on cross examination before the jury). When he went to prison for his part in the crimes, we did everything we could to protect his location, as well as his identity, but it somehow leaked about his true identity.
Details of a specific incident	The defendant referenced was residing in our District and case agents relocated the individual to another District.
Details of a specific incident	The defendant/witness referred to in this survey is the same person.
Procedures for protecting defendants; general comment about the frequency of harm	The district court has adopted split plea procedure by which cooperation agreements are protected. We have seen no change in the level of threats to witnesses and/or cooperating defendants based on this procedure.
Procedures for protecting witnesses; general comments about the sources to identify cooperator; general comment about the frequency of harm; general comment about harm in prison/prison culture	The [redacted] attempts to obtain protective orders in cases involving cooperating witnesses, and does not allow that information in the jails. Nonetheless, targets and defendants infer who the cooperators are from review of their discovery and spread the word about their cooperation in the jail. We have prosecuted two witness retaliation cases in the past three years, and have investigated several others. In the past several years, threats against cooperators have increased, and pre-trial separation orders have been ineffective in avoiding confrontations.
Procedures for protecting defendants; general comments about the sources to identify cooperator	The documents where it was apparent that someone was cooperating were filed under seal. However, sophisticated reviewers of docket entries usually presume that that means cooperation.

Categories	Open-Ended Comments
Nothing to report	The entire current staff of probation officers were polled. There were no other cases identified.
Details of a specific incident; general comment about harm in prison/prison culture; procedures for protecting defendants; general comment about the frequency of harm	The first case I mentioned involved very serious assaults on the defendant who provided useful cooperation relating to a number of cases. He was threatened and then beaten in two different prisons before finally being provided what appears to be secure housing. He was also in pretrial detention for many years in unacceptable segregated isolation because of the recognition he was in the process or would cooperate. (In my experience, defendants who cooperate during pretrial supervision often end up being housed in the most segregated and restrictive conditions.) This particular defendant's son, who was incarcerated in a state facility, was also threatened in connection with his father's cooperation. Viable threats were made against the family members also—who as a result had to move from their home. // The main pattern involved in other cases involves defendants who are in pretrial detention who face threats on the safety and welfare of the family members at home in [redacted] or [redacted] if they cooperate. We often do not end up knowing what happens under these circumstances. These defendants usually are too scared to even alert authorities regarding the threats. //
Takes issue with the survey; general comment about the frequency of harm; general comment about harm in prison/prison culture; general comments about the sources to identify cooperator; procedures for protecting defendants; policy comments	The format of this survey was troublesome for me because this is not a yes/no/# of cases issue. I don't have exact numbers, but I can say that in the last 5 years, the number of present and former clients who have demanded that I provide them their discovery or sentencing documents to show to other inmates to prove that they are not cooperating has skyrocketed. The demand to see PSR's is very high also, which causes problems for inmates because a lot of jails/prisons will not allow inmates to receive them in the mail. Many inmates are branded as snitches who are not actually cooperating, but there is often no way to prove that they are not cooperators. Additionally, a lot of my clients do not want to ask to go into PC because it is a horrible way to serve their sentences and the fact that they requested PC once will follow them around to other institutions and increase the likelihood that they will be placed their against their wills, for institutional safety. I honestly don't know how to balance a defendant's right to review the evidence against him with protecting him from harm based on suspicion, sometimes baseless, that he is cooperating.
General comment about the frequency of harm; procedures for protecting defendants; general comments about the sources to identify cooperator	The government regularly claims that cooperators are at risk but have never cited an example. AUSAs want files sealed to conceal cooperation agreements even AFTER the cooperators testified in open court in front of the defendant. Fear is rampant. I have a [redacted] participant who testified twice against a [co-conspirator] in a case which lasted more [than] [redacted]. She was never concerned.

Categories	Open-Ended Comments
Procedures for protecting defendants; policy comments	The harm or threats of harm experienced by my clients was directly related to the practice of one Judge who refused to seal documents in his cases and NOT to the practice or Local Rule with respect to sealing. This particular Judge's philosophy was 'this is a public courtroom, the public should have access.' As a consequence, and to avoid harm, many clients were advised of his practice and urged to factor that practice into the decision on whether or not to offer assistance.
Details of a specific incident	The last two cases, individuals went to the homes of defendants' families and threatened them, if defendant cooperated.
General comment about the frequency of harm; general comments about the sources to identify cooperator	The most common threats and attempted acts of harms, that I have encountered, occur when a defendant or a witness is a member of a well knit group of friends, gang members or connected families. Some of the acts of intimidation are not assisted by the contents of court orders, opinions or events in open court. Community knowledge of events is a common source of information about who is (or might be) allied with police or prosecution. But there are incidents where a witness or a defendant's role for the prosecution is uncovered only because lawyers and judges do not consider the danger to cooperators. There are general incentives (in gang cases) to promote a policy of harming snitches within local culture.
General comment about the frequency of harm; general comments about the sources to identify cooperator; details of a specific incident	The most frequent [occurrence] of threats is with cooperating non-defendant witnesses. Their cooperation is revealed through discovery: disclosure of immunity letters and interview reports. I had one witness kidnapped and beaten due to cooperation during investigation. Several other witnesses have been threatened once the witness list for trial is released.
Takes issue with the survey; general comment about the frequency of harm	The number 50 is a plug number because you would not accept a three figure number. These sorts of threats happen so routinely in gang and drug cases that i have lost count. The number of times I have become aware of such threats is EASILY in the hundreds.
General comment about the frequency of harm; procedures for protecting defendants; general comments about the sources to identify cooperator	The number of instances of threats were down in 2014 because the number of cases were down dramatically. Most defendants request that counsel alter court documents because inmates demand the plea agreements, court docket entries, and a [transcript] of the proceedings. If the inmate does not turn over the documents, they claim they are beaten. Sealing the documents would not be helpful in these cases. The larger problem is that co-defendants learn of cooperation against them and then disseminate the information to other co-defendants or unindicted co-conspirators. Mentally challenged defendants and older defendants seem to particularly be at risk.

Categories	Open-Ended Comments
Procedures for protecting defendants; general comment about the frequency of harm; general comments about the sources to identify cooperator	Additional comments provided over email: For more than three years we have following a practice of attaching a sealed supplement to every Statement in Advance of Plea regardless or whether there is a cooperation agreement or not. We do this to avoid it being apparent on the docket whether there is a cooperation agreement. Prior to our court adopting this practice, we received regular comments from counsel that defendants were subjected to threats and accusations once they arrived at the prison. I have not received similar comments since we adopted this practice. I hope this may be of help.
Takes issue with the survey; general comment about the frequency of harm; comments about refusal out of fear; procedures for protecting witnesses; general comments about the sources to identify cooperator; general comment about harm in prison/prison culture	The numbers listed above are only place holders to enable us to complete the survey. What numbers we do have and the relevant explanations are attached below. / / Not including the defendants regarding whom you've provided information in this survey, how many more defendants from cases prosecuted by your office have you learned were harmed or threatened in the past three years? / / 113 – This number is based on separation memos filed with the USMS to keep cooperators separated due to safety concerns and covers the years 2012 thru 2014. It may overstate the number of threats from co-defendants as most of these separation requests are based on concerns of AUSAs and may not necessarily involve an actual threat. / / Not including the witnesses regarding whom you've provided information in this survey, how many more witnesses from cases prosecuted by your office have you learned were harmed or threatened in the past three years? / / 22 – This number is based on the number of times the USAO provided assistance to witnesses to relocate due to concerns for their safety. This number probably under-estimates the actual number as it does not include those witnesses assisted by investigative agencies or witnesses who relocate on their own. / / / In the past three years, how many defendants withdrew offers of cooperation because of actual or threatened harm? / / While there is anecdotal evidence of defendants who withdraw offers of cooperation out of fear of retaliation, exact numbers are not known. But it is believed to be rare. / / In the past three years, how many defendants refused cooperation because of actual or threatened harm? / / We do not keep records of defendants who refuse to cooperate because of actual or threatened harm. However, regularly we do have defendants who offer to plead guilty and decline to cooperate in any way against their co-defendants for fear of retaliation. / / In the past three years, how many witnesses withdrew offers of cooperation because of actual or threatened harm? / / Again, we have no specific number; it does happen, but it is rare. / / In the past three years, how many witnesses refused cooperation because of actual or threatened harm? / / Unknown / / / Please use the space below to pro-

Categories	Open-Ended Comments
	vide any additional information about harm or threats of harm experienced by defendants and/or witnesses (or their family or friends) from cases prosecuted by your office in the past three years. / / In every case involving gangs, illegal narcotics, violent crime and now even some white collar crimes, our office is very sensitive to the safety of cooperators, be they defendants or witnesses. And while we don't currently have a specific system for tracking threats against cooperators, anecdotally, we know it happens regularly. / / In the last three years, the U.S. Attorney's Office has provided assistance in [redacted] different cases to witnesses and/or their families to temporarily or permanently relocate due to concern for their safety as a result of their cooperation with the government. And while not specific to the last three years, people have been murdered on suspicion of being a government witness, even when they were not. In the same time period, our office has sponsored [redacted] defendants to the Federal Witness Security Program, and we anticipate [redacted] more this year. / / There are several ways by which cooperation becomes known. The criminal element has its own intelligence system which can be very effective. In a recent case we learned members of a gang were accessing PACER to look for documents to confirm cooperation. The most common method to signal cooperation seems to be the delay between a guilty plea and sentencing. If the defendant is not sentenced in a timely manner and removed to BOP, he is suspected of cooperating and may be at risk. Even at BOP, inmates are demanding that newly arrived inmates provide copies of their plea agreements or transcripts of plea proceedings to verify they were not cooperators. / / At times, as a result of a motions hearing or of the discovery process, witness information is obtained. Most of the direct assistance to witness mentioned above [redacted] is a result of one of these two events. / /
Comments about refusal out of fear; details of a specific incident; general comments about the sources to identify cooperator; general comment about the frequency of harm	The offenders are reluctant to report the threats/harm to law enforcement since in some instances, the individuals reside in the same community; some have gone back to their prior criminal associates to seek support--could pose a risk to returning to the "gang lifestyle;" all incidents have been reported to federal or local authorities, but very little action has been taken; one offender asked for political [asylum] as threat was overseas; offenders are not aware of how the information "leaked and the threats are coming by way of messages sent by unknown individuals or means (e.g., unknown texts, callers).
Details of a specific incident; general comments about the sources to identify cooperator	The one case I recall involved a witness testifying at trial, and the threats came from defendant's family.

Categories	Open-Ended Comments
Details of a specific incident	The only cases reported as possible threats involved co-defendants (both female) who has been continuously threatened and abused throughout the course of the offense generally. Once they made the decision to cooperate, there were no further threats or intimidation, but the women remain fearful based on both actual and threatened harm to them during the course of the offense. There is nothing to indicate that the fact of their cooperation resulted in additional threats or actual harm in either case.
Details of a specific incident	The only incident I am aware of is the alleged murder of an FBI informant in a bank robbery case. I do not recall the details of how the informant's identity may have been disclosed. The U.S. Attorney never prosecuted the murder. He would have additional information that I do not have.
General comment about the frequency of harm	The only information the office has relative to threats are a number of allegations from defense attorneys that a client or family member was threatened. None of the allegations have been confirmed as being valid or related to the case being prosecuted.
Details of a specific incident	The prison guard was accused of "diming" the defendant. Never able to verify.
General comment about the frequency of harm; general comment about harm in prison/prison culture; general comments about the sources to identify cooperator	The rate of former clients (defendants) incarcerated at BOP facilities requesting copies of the their plea agreement, final judgment order, docket sheet, and sentencing transcripts, rose dramatically in calendar year 2014.
General comments about the sources to identify cooperator; general comment about the frequency of harm; procedures for protecting defendants; general comment about harm in prison/prison culture	The Rule 35 and 5K process is problematic. Our judges are resistant to routinely sealing these motions. We are increasingly hearing from cooperators about information taken from public filings being posted on sites such as "Who's a Rat". Additionally, threats to witnesses and cooperating defendants often result when the defendant learns from the discovery process that a particular co-defendant or witness is cooperating. Lately, we have begun hearing from cooperators in the BOP that when they leave their assigned institution on an ASR they are branded a cooperator and are retaliated against when they return.
Takes issue with the survey; general comment about the frequency of harm; comments about refusal out of fear; details of a specific incident; general comments about the sources to identify cooperator	The survey asked for overall numbers regarding harm or threats of harm to defendants and witnesses over the last three years. Our office does not have a system that captures such data, and therefore accurate numbers were difficult to collect. Individual Assistant United States Attorneys who are currently in the office tried to provide information based on their recollection of cases and incidents. Accordingly, we do not feel like we have an adequate quantitative result. Moreover, the actual numbers reported do not provide an adequate picture of the seriousness of the problem as, in our District, the fear of being identified as a cooperator because of fear of harm or retaliation has dramatically

Categories	Open-Ended Comments
	reduced the number of individuals willing to provide information to the government and testify against others. Indeed, the experience in our District is that we are unable to get individuals to cooperate because of their fear that something will happen to them or their family if they do. This seems to be an increasing problem over the years. One reason for this change is the increased focus on drug trafficking organizations with connections to [redacted]. Defendants and witnesses are worried about violence against themselves as well as their families in [redacted]. For example, one AUSA noted that in her last three cases that involved drug trafficking organizations that had connections to [redacted] (all large, multi-defendant cases, which used wiretaps), none of the defendants or putative defendants would cooperate for fear of retaliation against them or their families, both in [redacted] and [redacted]. In addition, in the violent crime cases, witnesses will often refuse to provide information, from the earliest stages of the investigation, to law enforcement for fear of retaliation. Even when we have had success in obtaining their testimony through grand jury testimony, these same witnesses will often refuse to testify at trial or will provide [a] different version at trial. The witnesses do not want to be perceived as cooperating with the government. / / Accordingly, in response to the questions above regarding how many witnesses and defendants refused cooperation because of actual or threatened harm, the answer that we want to provide is "many." A precise number is not available. It is very difficult for us to capture how many witnesses and defendants have told us that do not want to cooperate because of the risk. It seems to happen regularly in violent crime and drug trafficking cases. / / In addition, the stigma of being a cooperator/perceived as a cooperator seems to be so problematic that we have heard from defense counsel that even if their client/defendants provide safety valve proffers pursuant to USSG 5C1.2, they receive word from co-defendants/others in the organization that they are at risk of retaliation. The number of safety valve proffers has reduced dramatically, and the repercussions of refusal are less significant (since there has been a policy decision to apply few mandatory minimum sentences in drug cases). / / The document that most signals that someone is cooperating is a sealed plea agreement. If a plea agreement is sealed, it is a "red flag" alerting others that a particular defendant is cooperating, as there is no other reason to seal the plea agreement. / / Moreover, in most of our threat incidents, the cooperating witnesses/defendants were also identified through the discovery process. Many witnesses had to be moved for their safety. /

Categories	Open-Ended Comments
Details of a specific incident	The threats arose in a RICO case involving a gang. Some of the members of the gang cooperated with the Government, and they and their families were subjected to threats from the gang.
General comment about the frequency of harm	The threats I see only arise in (1) gun prosecutions of street gang members and (2) drug cases in which the witness or defendant has direct ties to [redacted] dealers.
Details of a specific incident; general comment about the frequency of harm	The threats involved were between rival families while a co-[defendant] who was a member of one family was cooperating against a member of another family during a co-[defendant's] trial. These types of threats are somewhat typical between the large extended families [redacted].
General comments about the sources to identify cooperator; details of a specific incident; general comment about the frequency of harm	The USAO for the [redacted] prosecutes major crimes committed by or against [redacted]. In such cases cooperators are readily identified by defendants and their families. This circumstance routinely leads to attempts to intimidate witnesses. Additionally, in at least one public corruption case from a [redacted] who cooperated with the government as a witness was the target of an attempt to oust him from office. That effort is believed to be motivated by a desire to retaliate against the witness for his cooperation. / / /
Details of a specific incident; general comment about the frequency of harm; policy comments; procedures for protecting defendants; general comments about the sources to identify cooperator	The worst case I had involved the murder of several family members of two defendants (mother and son) to punish them for losing a substantial amount of contraband and also to intimidate them into not cooperating. Credible threats against defendants are frequent. I do not recall a precise number, but they are credible enough to keep the defendant from cooperating and receiving a lower sentence. Additional comments provided over phone: Respondent completed the survey with information, but he really focused on the last year and not the last three years. He said he feels like this happens 2-4 times per year in his district, and it is most often the defendants. Defendants will qualify for the "safety valve" but then not take it out of concern of being harmed. He suggested that the committees consider two levels for a filing system. Current CM/ECF only protects information through sealing. The sealed event still provides a record, and drug traffickers know how to read the dockets for what this sealed information is really saying. If there were a public version and a private version of the docket you could better protect the information. Sealing everything just triggers an alarm. He had a case involving a drug conspiracy where the main defendant was the brother of a high level member of a drug cartel. He told his lawyer he would not cooperate because he was concerned about the safety of his family and his

Categories	Open-Ended Comments
	wife's family back [redacted]. The lawyer had the [redacted] contact people in [redacted] to obtain information about the cartel [redacted]. This information was provided to federal authorities so the defendant could receive the benefits of cooperation. Nothing was ever signed, and the judge was made aware of the cooperation only through conversations with counsel, both prosecution and defense. If there were a private version of the docket this information could be recorded, even noted in a pre-sentence report.
General comment about the frequency of harm; details of a specific incident; general comments about the sources to identify cooperator; procedures for protecting defendants	There are frequently threats of harm to defendants' families since my docket is close to [redacted]. In specific cases, such as the [redacted] trial, there were threats to defendants, witnesses, families, etc. In the gang conspiracy cases, there are usually threats to defendants, witnesses and family members. I am not aware of any documents [identifying] any person individually, but, of course, I do not know what happens once the BOP gets custody. All 5K motions and orders are filed as are Rule 35 motions and orders and Pre-sentencing memos are also sealed at sentencings, but have to be unsealed for appeal and other post sentencing actions.
Nothing to report	There has been no actual physical harm to a defendant to my knowledge. Defendants are more concerned with perceived harm and very few [ever] receive an actual threat of harm.
General comment about harm in prison/prison culture; general comment about the frequency of harm; general comments about the sources to identify cooperator; procedures for protecting defendants	There is a disconnect in the Bureau of Prisons between Washington senior management and the experience on the ground. I believe senior management has expressed the view that harm to cooperators while incarcerated is minimal. We have a federal prison in the district and have talked to the warden. He has indicated that the problem is significant and half of his [Special] Housing population consists of cooperators in protective custody. There are also a variety of other means those intent on harming cooperators are using to gather cooperation data. I presume there will be space elsewhere in the survey to report those findings. Additional comments provided in email: Those who are seeking to identify and verify cooperation of various defendants are extremely sophisticated. They are using a variety of means to gather information. By way of example, they are requiring incarcerated, suspected cooperators to obtain a copy of their judgment and turn it over to the prison gangs. There is apparently no BOP policy precluding this. They are requiring cooperator members' families to obtain transcripts and judgments so that they can compare sentencing exposure with sentencing results, and such documents clearly reflect cooperation without expressly saying so. In this District, we are using all means at our disposal to refrain from disclosing cooperation, including sealed doc-

Categories	Open-Ended Comments
	uments, sealed proceedings and attachments to the judgment, among others. However, those protocols are not eliminating the problem. There is also a developing trend in our Circuit jurisprudence that seems oblivious to the cooperation issue. We do not discuss cooperation in the context of a plea, but we fully recognize that the prospect of a cooperation departure is a prime motivating factor for the plea. The Circuit has issued some opinions that question the absence of such a conversation during the Rule 11 plea colloquy. This entire problem is national in scope, and would benefit from a national policy. However, if there continues to be a disconnect between BOP's national management and prison officials on the ground, I am not sure that any policy will alleviate the problem.
General comment about harm in prison/prison culture; general comment about the frequency of harm	There seems to be an organized effort in the BOP by some inmates to determine whether other inmates have/are cooperating. We have received an uptick in former clients wanting information to prove they didn't cooperate.
General comments about the sources to identify cooperator; procedures for protecting defendants	There were direct threats to me and my family that the Marshall addressed. If there are closed sentencing hearing it is presumed that it is to discuss cooperation. I don't mention the [cooperation] agreement on the record or close a sentencing hearing unless specifically requested by the parties. Attorneys regularly [practicing] before me understand this and it works well. There are always reasons for a variance regardless of cooperation. Newer attorneys want to discuss the cooperation agreement in detail and we have to close the hearing. It is no secret after that.
Nothing to report	There were none in 2013 or 2014
Takes issue with the survey; general comment about the frequency of harm; comments about refusal out of fear	These are not all-inclusive. Exact numbers can't be known. The "no snitching" culture is strong in [redacted]. We have not kept statistics on this, but many witnesses and defendants fear to cooperate without identifying their reasons.
Takes issue with the survey; comments about refusal out of fear	these cases are difficult to follow. The clients stop talking to us when they get really scared
General comments about the sources to identify cooperator; general comment about harm in prison/prison culture	They have access to PACER at the prisons and so prisoners and/or guards go through the dockets and tell people what the charges were and what the sentences were. This leads to being able to figure out if they cooperated.
Takes issue with the survey	This entire survey is a waste of time.
General comment about the frequency of harm; comments about refusal out of fear; procedures for protecting witnesses; procedures for protecting defendants	This is [redacted] and many defendants have links to DTOs. As such, defendants often have to balance the possibility of threats against the possibility of reduced sentences. Indeed, AUSAs in our district believed that the perceived or potential of threat or harm (without any actual threat made or harm inflicted) deters many defendants from cooperat-

Categories	Open-Ended Comments
	ing and/or inhibits them from following through with the cooperation addendum. In addition, we were involved with several incidents in 2014 in which cooperators had to be relocated or placed in WITSEC due to threats. Finally, we also would note that, several years ago, our district court developed a docketing system, in consultation with USAO and FPD, to endeavor to better protect cooperators entering pleas. Called the Master Sealed Event calendar, it creates a docket skip early in every case, and then going forward a separate cooperation addendum gets appended, without a docket skip, to a special sealed calendar.
Policy comments; general comment about harm in prison/prison culture; general comments about the sources to identify cooperator; general comment about the frequency of harm	This is not a problem the judiciary can solve by sealing court records because inmates are required to "prove" they have not cooperated by producing their own paperwork. If the inmate has cooperated, which is often the case, he simply has no choice but to check himself into the Segregated Housing Unit because he knows the other inmates will access PACER and learn that he has cooperated. I have even had requests from defendants and attorneys to seal a defendant's entire court file so no member of the public could access it. Even then, however, the sealing of court documents related to sentencing raises a red flag as to whether a particular defendant has cooperated. This is a serious problem that needs to be promptly addressed by the DOJ. Defendants do not understand when they enter a plea and cooperation agreement that they are likely agreeing to serve their sentence in solitary confinement. Many of these inmates serve years in the SHU and if they are transferred to another institution the process simply starts over again and they enter the SHU for their own protection at the new institution. Although this is a DOJ/BOP problem, the judiciary has an interest in it because judges accept these pleas and they sentence defendants pursuant to the pleas. A sentence served in the SHU is a very different sentence than one served in general population. There is no programming. Any inmate serving a lengthy sentence in the SHU stands little if any chance at rehabilitation. The judiciary should insist the DOJ address this increasing problem.
Takes issue with the survey	This is useless when the relative of a defendant was murdered.
General comment about the frequency of harm; Takes issue with the survey	This issue is raised continually by defense counsel but I have no evidence of actual harm resulting. However, I lose track of cases after sentencing, so I am not the best person to ask.
Details of a specific incident	This response only represents one case.

Categories	Open-Ended Comments
General comment about the frequency of harm; general comment about harm in prison/prison culture; general comments about the sources to identify cooperator	Threats against actual or perceived cooperators are very common. There is hardly a drug case where the ones caught with the drugs (or their families) are not threatened by leaders of the drug trafficking organizations. Others in the jail suspect cooperators when they get pulled from the facility and brought for a debrief. The government often discloses to codefendants the cooperation of one in order to coerce guilty pleas. I have never had a case where cooperation was learned from the filing of any document or something said in the courtroom. A person's cooperation is usually discovered or suspected long before the govt files a 5K1.1 or Rule 35 motion.
General comments about the sources to identify cooperator	Threats have been made after release of [discovery] (particularly Jencks).
General comment about the frequency of harm; general comment about harm in prison/prison culture; details of a specific incident; procedures for protecting defendants; procedures for protecting witnesses	Threats lower because our caseload has dropped since US Atty doesn't bring many cases here (he prefers [redacted] with lesser penalties). At BOP, prisoners often demand to see PSR or dkt sheet to alert them to prior cooperation. It's dangerous to give up documents and dangerous not to. One of my trials was against killers of a witness. Cooperators often face disapproving and threatening family and former friends when they get up on the stand. It causes some to be very cautious and not especially good witnesses. Family estrangement is a strong motivator to keep silent. A number of my defendants or cooperators are in WitSec and/or protective BOP custody.
General comment about the frequency of harm; general comment about harm in prison/prison culture; procedures for protecting defendants; general comments about the sources to identify cooperator	Threats of harm and harm to inmates are not limited to cooperators. Sex offenders and clients who victimize children receive some of the worst threats and injuries. It is very common for inmates to request sentencing documents to prove they are not cooperators or sex offenders. When an inmate arrives on a housing unit in a BOP facility they are required to prove they are not a snitch or a sex offender. If they do not or cannot prove they have "clean paper" they have to request protective custody. Many of these clients end up serving their sentences in the most restrictive conditions with no access to treatment or other programs. They live in fear even in protective custody. The prisons are so understaffed that prison [authorities] rely on inmates to keep order. This system of social stratification is therefore tolerated if not condoned. While PACER and CM/ECF have conferred great benefits they also have made life much more difficult for many inmates. Many inmates have someone on the outside with access to PACER to verify the status of other inmates. It is not hard to spot a snitch or a sex offender if you have access to PACER.

Categories	Open-Ended Comments
General comment about the frequency of harm	Threats of harm are often recited to me from defendants during sentencing but rarely do I have any method of verifying their reliability. I do not doubt, however, that retribution for cooperation is a serious concern for many defendants faced with the Hobson's choice of cooperating or not receiving the most favorable plea agreement or the 5K or Rule 35 motion essential for avoiding the minimum mandatory sentence.
General comment about the frequency of harm; general comments about the sources to identify cooperator; general comment about harm in prison/prison culture; procedures for protecting defendants	Threats of harm to cooperators are routine in our principal pretrial detention facility and at various BOP [institutions]. Cooperators are sometimes identified through discovery documents when the case goes to trial (or very close to trial). We have reports of defendants (whether they cooperated or not) being told to provide sentencing and/or plea transcripts to prove to others at a BOP facility that they did not cooperate. Cooperators sometimes also are identified (or believed to be identified) through J&C's that contain a sentence not seeming consistent with the charges. We limit access to some documents sent to the BOP by requiring that they be viewed in the Warden's Office (or some other restricted space).
General comment about the frequency of harm; procedures for protecting defendants	Threats of harm usually made to cooperators while they are in pretrial detention with co-defendants. A request is then made to transfer to another detention center or to a different area of the present detention center. These requests are almost always granted.
General comment about the frequency of harm; general comments about the sources to identify cooperator	Threats seem to occur more often when the Govt. lets co-defendants know that a cooperator will testify at trial. At sentencing, threats against cooperators [are] used to strengthen the Govt's 5K1 motion on behalf of the cooperator.
General comment about the frequency of harm	Threats that I am aware of were addressed either to me or to the prosecutor in a given case. I am unaware of any witness that has been threatened, and I have not received any reports from the Bureau of Prisons of harm done to a cooperating defendant/inmate.
General comment about the frequency of harm	Threats to co-defendants, witnesses and victims have occurred in assault, rape, child sexual abuse and drug conspiracy cases. Threats of harm are a particular problem in [redacted] cases.
General comment about the frequency of harm; policy comments	threats to cooperating co-defendants are reported fairly frequently but I do not know if they are real threats or just talk. It often appears to be just talk. It is hard to solve the problem, because the identity of the cooperating co-defendant or witness usually cannot be kept from the defendant, who is usually the perceived source of the threat.
General comment about the frequency of harm	Threats to victims, witnesses and cooperating defendants has been increasing each year.
Nothing to report	to my knowledge [there] have been no threats

Categories	Open-Ended Comments
Details of a specific incident; general comments about the sources to identify cooperator	Two co-defendants were beaten in pre-trial detention when discovery/Jencks statements were given to defendants in jail and they learned of the co-defendants' cooperation. / An informant was killed when a gang learned he was informing to law enforcement.
Details of a specific incident; procedures for protecting defendants	Two multi-defendant [redacted] cases in parallel prosecutions in which each had one or more cooperators and one in each case had veiled or express threats of violence or physical harm to the [cooperating] defendant or his family members which resulted in permission for each of the threatened families to relocate to another state pending completion of the case. The case ultimately ended with each/all of the defendants entering pleas of guilty and the last of them was sentenced [redacted].
General comment about the frequency of harm	Uncertain of number, but there are a few cases that have been verbally threatened.
Procedures for protecting defendants	Usually the government and defense counsel have an agreed upon approach to these matters.
General comment about the frequency of harm; procedures for protecting defendants; general comment about harm in prison/prison culture; comments about refusal out of fear	Very few defendants ever tell me about threats or harm once they are sentenced. I have had a [few] (maybe 3-5) letters from prisons saying they are being threatened. In those situations we tell the AUSA or probation. Roughly half of the clients who could cooperate choose not to. A portion of these are concerned about their [safety].
Takes issue with the survey	Very hard to predict on a case [by] case basis.
General comment about the frequency of harm; general comment about harm in prison/prison culture	Virtually every defendant that we represent who ends up in BOP custody calls us to request proof that the defendant did not cooperate. Each inmate tells the same story -- he is confronted shortly after arrival at a BOP facility by an inmate or inmates saying that he has x number of days to prove he is not a cooperator or he will be beaten. Defendants routinely ask us to do things we cannot do -- i.e., provide a fake docket entry, fake statement of reasons for sentence, or to buy transcripts revealing the lack of cooperation.
Procedures for protecting defendants; policy comments; general comment about harm in prison/prison culture	We are not allowed to provide copies of discovery and pre sentence reports to defendants detained due to potential threats of harm. However, this prohibition limits the defendant's ability to thoroughly review the evidence against them. / Often, once the Defendant has been sentenced I have no further contact so I may not know if cooperation has [led] to threats of harm once in BOP custody.
Details of a specific incident	We can only recall one other case approximately 6 years ago where a cooperator was assaulted due to his cooperation while in pretrial detention.

Categories	Open-Ended Comments
General comment about the frequency of harm; general comment about harm in prison/prison culture; general comments about the sources to identify cooperator	We constantly hear from clients about their desire to have documents to use in BOP to prove they are not cooperating. That number is in the hundreds. Media coverage of sentencings on TV leads to threats and violence against our clients. They are [savvy] enough to know that a sentence is too low following a guilty plea without cooperation.
Takes issue with the survey; nothing to report	We do not track this information so I cannot answer these questions with a specific number so I had to put 0.
General comment about the frequency of harm; general comment about harm in prison/prison culture; general comments about the sources to identify cooperator	We do not track this information, so my numbers understate the occurrence. There has been a large increase in numbers of defendants calling or writing from BOP asking for their docket sheet. It is clear that most of the time it is because they are being pressured to produce this info to other prisoners. In one instance, another prisoner could be heard in the background telling my client what to ask for. / However, we don't track our defendants once they get to BOP, so we would not normally receive information about threats within BOP. Defendants who come back to us on Supervised Release Violations after release relate that this practice of checking docket sheets inside BOP is very common.
General comment about the frequency of harm; procedures for protecting witnesses	We experience this difficulty all the time, and constantly spend funds moving witnesses.
Details of a specific incident; procedures for protecting defendants	We found two cases that fit the criteria of the [survey]. The first case is outlined above. Basically, the defendant was on bond and while he was on bond, he was working as a confidential informant. While on bond, he reported receiving death threats and was relocated for a time. He was in protective custody by A.T.F. So while he was on pretrial release we know he received death threats. We found out that after the defendant was on supervision by the probation office he was shot to death at a local bar. The second case involved a defendant reported being intimidated but not threatened. He reported a truck would drive by his house and park there and watch him. He noted several individuals also approached him and asked him questions about his family.
Procedures for protecting defendants; general comments about the sources to identify cooperator; policy comments	We generally seal plea agreements with cooperation provisions, but it is an unsatisfactory approach. Inmates have become sophisticated in reading PACER, and many understand that a "sealed event" around the time of the plea is a strong indicator that the defendant is cooperating. This issue is of great concern to us, and we welcome the attention that is being paid to it.

Categories	Open-Ended Comments
General comment about the frequency of harm; details of a specific incident; general comment about harm in prison/prison culture	We have a large number of gun and drug cases that arise in the inner cities and often with gang involvement. It is very common for witnesses in these communities to experience threats and intimidation. In several state prosecutions witnesses have been harmed and in some cases murdered. We have not had any witnesses murdered but it is not uncommon for a [witness] to report that fellow gang members have made threatening remarks to them. In one of the cases referenced earlier a witness was confronted at the door to her house by a man with a gun threatening her and her son because her son was a witness to a shooting and warning not to talk to the authorities. Threats and assaults in jail on cooperating defendants or those thought to be cooperating is not uncommon.
General comment about the frequency of harm; general comment about harm in prison/prison culture; general comments about the sources to identify cooperator; procedures for protecting defendants; procedures for protecting witnesses; details of a specific incident	We have a lot of anecdotal evidence from defense counsel that defendants are being confronted in BOP facilities based on cooperation (documents from PACER like 5K or Rule 35 motions, or even cooperation paragraphs in plea agreements), however, counsel have been reluctant to give us specifics about those threats. Many of our cases start out with the state, and defendants use documents from the state case, like complaints or search warrants, to find out who is cooperating and retaliate against them. Additional comments provided over phone: Respondent noted that his district sees a lot of harm to defendants and witnesses, but court documents, at least PACER documents, are rarely the source. Defenders know this to be an issue as well, and they were responding to the survey in the same way. Respondent then provided a brief description of how criminal cases work in his district. Even in purely federal cases, which he noted are quite rare for them, the prosecution is required early on to provide statements and plea agreements as part of discovery (within two weeks of the arraignment, by local rule). So these documents (5K, Rule 35, etc.) are given to the defense as part of discovery. The documents are sometimes the source of the information, but are RARELY obtained through PACER. Even if the name of the cooperator or witness is not included, the defendant often can figure out the name of the person based on the information (e.g., the sale of drugs on a specific day or at a specific place tells them who the buyer was). Respondent then relayed more information about the case he mentioned in his email contact. A multi-conviction drug dealer was under state investigation again. A search warrant was left as part of the investigation, so even before discovery, and from that information he was able to obtain the name of the cooperator, who he later lured onto the railroad tracks and shot. This is now a federal case. The only solution to preventing defendants from getting this kind of information is to seek a protective order, which the prosecutors almost never do be-

Categories	Open-Ended Comments
	cause they are difficult to obtain. The district does try to protect cooperation information by entering 5K and Rule 35 information orally during a sentencing hearing (after notifying the court via email that such information will be entered), so there is no PACER docket entry for this. However, if someone went to the trouble of paying to obtain the transcript, they could learn it from there.
Procedures for protecting defendants	We have a procedure in place in the [redacted] to protect cooperating defendants. We have created a master sealed event in all criminal cases except immigration cases. This is where the attorneys can have docketed any matters relating to cooperation. It seems to work well.
General comments about the sources to identify cooperator	We have been informed of assumptions by outside individuals that anything sealed or any missing ECF docket numbers covers a sealed document that relates to cooperation.
General comment about the frequency of harm; general comments about the sources to identify cooperator; policy comments	We have experienced a distinct uptick in threatened and actual violence to witnesses and cooperator/targets in the last ten years. Drug traffickers are using their networks as well as [following] docket entries for sealed filings, transfer motions and waivers of pretrial motions. We believe a more secure system for filing sensitive pleading should be developed. There is also a "paralegal" who monitors some of the more significant drug cases. This [paralegal] is seen speaking with the defendants as well as the defense lawyers. Defense counsel do not welcome the input of the paralegal.
Details of a specific incident; general comments about the sources to identify cooperator; general comment about harm in prison/prison culture	We have had a "certified complex" drug conspiracy case where a codefendant was afraid for his life for cooperating with agents. This case has not been sentenced yet. There was no plea agreement or 5K filed (yet), but there was a debrief with this codefendant who implicated other codefendants. This codefendant was assaulted for no reason while in custody pending sentence for the instant case and believes the leader/organizer of this conspiracy ordered the assault. / / In the past three years, we have reviewed about 3 PSRs where the material witnesses in alien smuggling cases were threatened harm if they talked to agents concerning the defendant. Names of material witnesses are disclosed in PSR's with their statement regarding the defendant and the instant offense. It is unknown if the defendant actually carried out the threat of harm as most or all of these material witnesses in these types of cases are deported before the defendant is sentenced. No additional information about these cases is known. /
General comment about the frequency of harm; general comment about harm in prison/prison culture; general comments about the sources to identify cooperator	We have had multiple reports that defendants in BOP custody are routinely asked to "show papers," meaning J&C, PSR, transcripts of plea and sentencing hearings, etc., and that if they could not or did not they were targeted for violence. In the case of at least one facility, this was confirmed by a Correctional Officer.

Categories	Open-Ended Comments
General comment about the frequency of harm	We have other cases where the defendant/offender has indicated they were threatened by others do to the cooperation but no evidence of the validity of the threat or how others became aware of his cooperation.
Nothing to report	We know of no harm or threats of harm in 2013 or 2014.
General comment about the frequency of harm; comments about refusal out of fear	We know that sometimes witnesses and cooperators refuse to cooperate due to threats or perceived threats, but that information is not always communicated to us. Also, the threats of harm or harm may not be the sole reason to refuse the cooperation.
General comment about the frequency of harm; procedures for protecting defendants	We prosecute a large number of cases in this district that depend on the cooperation of defendants and witnesses who have reason to fear retaliation or have been actually threatened. We do not track this information; therefore the numbers above are not reliable. There are merely a guess, but it is a substantial number each year. We are [redacted] and prosecute a large number of cartel and gang cases. This is a factor in every case. And, in almost every case, the fear of retaliation or the actual threats are made against cooperators or family members in [redacted], complicating matters substantially more than where the cooperators and/or their family members are entirely [redacted].
General comment about the frequency of harm; general comments about the sources to identify cooperator; general comment about harm in prison/prison culture	We receive frequent requests for sentencing transcripts from incarcerated defendants who have no appeal or habeas pending. These requests appear to be from defendants who are being pressured/threatened to demonstrate to other inmates that they did not cooperate with the government. Although I have no information of actual threats, I have a strong impression that this is a major problem for incarcerated inmates, whether or not they actually cooperated.
General comment about the frequency of harm; procedures for protecting defendants	We take extra precaution to try to prevent harm but it is sometimes inevitable.
Takes issue with the survey; general comment about harm in prison/prison culture; general comment about the frequency of harm; general comments about the sources to identify cooperator	You are asking the wrong person when you ask my office. We represent the LEAD defendant who is usually the person being snitched on, not the person doing the snitching. That said, we do regularly receive requests from defendants in the BOP for PSRs to prove they did not cooperate. We also occasionally receive requests to doctor documents to show cooperators did not cooperate.

Categories	Open-Ended Comments
Procedures for protecting defendants; general comment about harm in prison/prison culture; general comments about the sources to identify cooperator; policy comments; general comment about the frequency of harm	We used to have mandatory plea agreement supplements that were sealed and filed in every case in an attempt to make it more difficult to tell which defendants were cooperating. Defense counsel reported that this was putting all defendants in jeopardy (including the people who did not cooperate) because the sealed docket entry suggested to fellow inmates that the defendant had cooperated. Accordingly, we stopped the practice of mandatory plea agreement supplements. Presently, motions for downward departure and cooperation agreements are automatically sealed documents. The docket entries are not visible to the public, but the docket will reflect a skipped number, which we are told is a signal to those who might wish to harm a cooperating defendant. Sealed cooperation-related documents are sealed for the duration of a defendant's term of incarceration. Counsel may move to seal things like sentencing memos which contain references to cooperation. On an adequate showing, those motions to seal are routinely granted. Our court has spent significant amount of time discussing this issue, and we have decided to await national guidance on the best way to balance the important interests at stake.
General comment about the frequency of harm	When defendants request reductions of their sentences under Rule 35, they and their lawyers generally contend that the defendants have been threatened, but I have no documented cases of such threats.
General comment about the frequency of harm; procedures for protecting defendants	While defendants at times ask for entire plea agreements to be sealed or not even docketed because of a perceived threat, I have never had any defendant or defense counsel or government attorney provide any details to support the perception.
General comment about the frequency of harm; details of a specific incident; general comments about the sources to identify cooperator; general comment about harm in prison/prison culture	While I don't have additional information about actual harm or actual threats of harm, I am frequently reminded of the dangers for offenders of being associated with the Government. In one recent large, multi-defendant heroin distribution case in which some defendants had gang affiliations, virtually every defendant [redacted] requested a copy of the transcript of his sentencing. This was not done for appeal purposes - because in each case the appeal period had run when the request was made. My court reporter told me that, in several cases, she was advised by the person requesting (and paying for) the transcript that the transcript was needed so that the defendant could show to other inmates that he was not a "snitch."

Categories	Open-Ended Comments
General comment about the frequency of harm; Takes issue with the survey	While not many AUSAs in the district advised that they experienced defendants or witnesses experiencing harm or threats in the last three years, the AUSA who serves as the district's Professional Responsibility Officer (PRO) and Appellate Chief advised that he has heard of plenty of instances surrounding these issues in his capacity as PRO and Appellate Chief. Therefore, we submit that even though AUSAs may not be quantifying these situations in their daily casework, the issues do arise and the PRO and/or appellate division may be another good source for information. / / Note, that we entered 0 to the questions above because the approximate numbers, if any, are unknown.
General comment about the frequency of harm	While we have had a few [defendants] over the past three years express fears for their safety after cooperating with the government, these fears were based on the nature of the cooperation and no direct or indirect threats were made.
General comment about the frequency of harm; general comments about the sources to identify cooperator; comments about refusal out of fear	Within the District, there is a general perception that cooperators will be harmed, even if there is no specific credible threat of harm known. Even use of the safety valve provision is generally rejected by defendants in narcotics cases given their understanding that said provision could lead to the label of cooperator and the perceived risks that entails. Many defendants do not even consider cooperation or even the safety valve as a result.
Policy comments; general comments about the sources to identify cooperator; procedures for protecting defendants	Additional comments provided over email: If the survey is like other FJC surveys, I expect there will be opportunity for open-ended comments. That will be important to me. I have very strong feelings about what the Judiciary should and should not be willing to do in this arena. We are obviously all concerned about threats, intimidation and actual harm inflicted on a defendant who chooses to cooperate. We should get real, hard data on how extensive the problem is. Right now, I hear lots of anecdotes, but have very little real, hard information. This will be a good first step. But even if the survey develops hard data of a genuine and significant problem, I think the Judiciary must be very cautious about compromising the transparency and accuracy of Court records to address the problem. I don't have any problem with Courts doing what we have always done: namely, make case specific decision on whether and what to file under seal. But the recent proposals I've heard go way beyond that and would, if adopted, involve scrubbing the docket entirely of all references to the filing of Rule 35 or 5K motions (not just sealing content in appropriate cases), and in some instances even filing a public version of a plea agreement that appears to be complete but really isn't because there is a private, undisclosed rider that covers cooperation and substantial assistance.

Categories	Open-Ended Comments
	In my view, adoption of proposals like these last two go way beyond sealing records in appropriate cases, and actually strike at the core of the transparency and accountability that is so essential to the integrity and operation of the Court. Court records should, in my view, fairly reflect what actually happened in a case. If there was a Rule 35 or 5K departure motion filed, the record needs to reflect that, even if the content of the motions is sealed for good cause. Otherwise, the Court is publishing a docket that distorts the reality of what occurred in a case. Similarly, if there is a Plea Agreement with a cooperation provision, and that is actually part of the plea deal, the record should not falsely suggest that there is Plea Agreement without such a cooperation provision. The proposal I've heard to file a public version of a Plea Agreement that does not include the cooperation provision, when everyone involved realizes the real deal actually does include cooperation, would in my view put the Judiciary in the position of creating a false and misleading record of what is actually occurring. And obviously I don't think the Judiciary should countenance that sort of thing. Making individualized decisions to seal some or all of the content of a document is perfectly proper and well-established judicial practice in my view. It does result in some compromise of the normal, presumptive right of public access to Court records. But the compromise is appropriate when a judicial officer determines there is good cause for the sealed filing. But the proposals that go beyond this, and that would distort the judicial record of what is actually happening in a case are totally different in my view. At least in my District, I'm hearing the US Attorney's Office--often with support from the Defender Service--push for the more extreme record scrubbing that would, in my view distort the reality of what is happening in a case. I understand and applaud the desire to protect people who choose to cooperate. But I don't think that protection can or should come at the expense of the integrity of the Court record.
Details of a specific incident; general comments about the sources to identify cooperator; procedures for protecting defendants; Procedures for protecting witnesses; Takes issue with the survey	Additional comments provided over email: I have the following information to report regarding threats or harm to offenders due to their cooperation: 1) [redacted] - was prosecuted for threatening a material witness [redacted]- see below. 2) [redacted] - was threatened by [redacted] regarding her testimony against [redacted]. [redacted] threatened with physical harm to herself and her family. No actual harm was done. [redacted] was on pretrial release at the time of the threat. No information to indicate she requested protective custody or that she received same. No information to indicate that court documents were used to identify the defendant as a cooperator.

Categories	Open-Ended Comments
	3) [redacted] is being prosecuted for witness tampering. He made a series of phone calls to people to attempt to dissuade them from testifying in the sentencing of [redacted]. No information to indicate there were actual threats made. Defendant was in custody for TSR revocation at the time. Witnesses were in the community and no information is available about the witnesses requesting protection. No threat of physical or financial harm was reported and none actually occurred. Discovery material (statements) was disseminated amongst several people in this case. 4) [redacted] has received various threats of physical harm to him and his family due to his cooperation against other defendants. Some co-defendants distributed discovery material which included statements provided by [redacted]. [redacted] was on bond at the time of the treats and it has continued to his time on probation. No harm has actually occurred to date. 5) [redacted] is a [redacted] who cooperated with the Government against other [redacted]. He has been detained and awaiting sentencing since [redacted]. He is trying to enter the BOP Witness Security Program. We have no specific threat information, but there is a sincere concern for his safety. Please let me know if you have any questions or require additional information. I took the request to mean that we had to compile one response for the entire district so I did not complete the form itself.
Takes issue with the survey; general comment about the frequency of harm; details of a specific incident; general comment about harm in prison/prison culture; procedures for protecting defendants; general comments about the sources to identify cooperator	Additional comments provided over email: I have been attempting to complete the survey "Cooperators – Federal defenders and CJA Panel representatives" I am [redacted]. [redacted]. I truly appreciate your efforts in gathering information useful to the courts for this very real problem. I have attempted to complete the survey as constructed which has a number difficulties in getting useful information for the courts. I understand researchers like check box surveys because they can be more easily "scored" than interviews or open ended questions. However the issues are much more complex than what will be revealed by the structure of the questions asked. Despite that I dutifully went through the series of questions but got an error message "you cannot continue until you enter a valid number." This came with the following series of questions: 1. "In the past three years, how many defendants, because of actual or threatened harm, requested case information (CM/ECF docket, pre-sentence report, etc.) to prove they were not a cooperator?" 2. "In the past three years, how many defendants, because of actual or threatened harm, requested all or part of their CM/ECF docket be sealed?"

Categories	Open-Ended Comments
	3. "In the past three years, how many defendants withdrew offers of cooperation because of actual or threatened harm?"
	The answer to #1 — There was a large space to answer (as there was in the other two) so I thought I could type in an explanation. My answer was: "This happens so routinely I cannot give a number. Most defendants are shaken down for case information upon arrival at BOP institution. This is 100% of defendants who are assigned to a USP and some that go to a medium." This has been the case for nearly my entire career. I do not have a number and would have to pull case files to get a number. The form wants a number. I put it at 75%. It would not take 75% This error warning (as the other two error warnings) did not come until I had completed all three of the questions.
	The answer to #2 was "None that I can recall. I have suggested this and been told it will not help and will actually raise a red flag and cause everyone to believe defendant was cooperator if items are sealed." The form wants a number so I put "0" (i.e. zero.) Form wouldn't take it.
	The answer to #3 was "This averages about 30%." This percentage is the defendants who are, no matter what, going to a USP versus a medium or lower. Form would not take answer or 30%.
	The last questions about the number of defendants/or witnesses harmed or threatened due to perceived or actual cooperation with the government higher or lower in 2014 vs 2013. I would answer lower because I have been told by defendants that they have learned that it does not get them anywhere and actually can make it worse if they complain.
	As for additional information (an open ended question) I can state the following:
	In addition to criminal defense work I do civil rights cases and FTCA cases. I frequently receive requests from inmates to represent them in cases where they have been seriously assaulted (usually with homemade knives) by fellow inmates. Due to the technical legal difficulties with §1983 cases and FTCA cases, and the expense and time necessary to take on such a case, I and other lawyers routinely turn down these requests for representation. I am currently in [redacted] on one such case that I did take regarding an individual who was assaulted so badly (because he was believed to be a snitch) that he had to have a kidney surgically removed, had heart repair surgery and is missing part of a lung. [redacted] because even without discovery the courts have so far held that "discretionary function" exception bars the suit. Some institutions are better run than others and can protect prisoners better than others. The perpetrators of this vicious assault received very minor sentences attached to their current sentences. There is no deterrence

Categories	Open-Ended Comments
	of perpetrators of assaults nor any real threat of any ramifications for prison officials who fail to adequately protect prisoners at risk.
	As for district judges and protecting cooperators and others the situation is this: Every plea agreement in [redacted] for years has the following three required paragraphs that must be agreed to by the defendant:
	[redacted]
	These paragraphs are not in every district. Ironically the "debrief" required is often not bothered with or is cursory and does not provide any new information. However the paragraphs create obvious problems for the defendant when incarcerated.
	I hope this helps with your research. I hope that interviews of CJA district representatives, and FPDs and AFPDs are being contemplated in the future. In addition to criminal defense counsel who have represented defendants and witnesses who have been assaulted, civil rights attorneys who have represented similar victims are being contemplated.
General comment about the frequency of harm; general comment about harm in prison/prison culture; procedures for protecting defendants; policy comments; general comments about the sources to identify cooperators; details of a specific incident	Additional comments provided over email: Some weeks ago I returned your committee's survey on threats or harm to witnesses. At the time, I was personally familiar with only one or two cases. By coincidence the issue came up in connection with a request to unseal plea agreements that would indicate who had cooperated. The United States Attorney [redacted] presented three witnesses, with national and local experience, who effectively described the range of problems that occur when a cooperating witness is identified. The witnesses gave numerous examples of retaliation against cooperating witnesses, those merely suspected of cooperating, and even those who spoke to prison officials to give exculpatory information about a suspect. [Redacted]
Details of a specific incident; general comment about harm in prison/prison culture	[Case transcript provided over email]